LILIANE & FRED FUNCKEN

Arms and Uniforms · 2

18th Century to the present day

WARD LOCK LIMITED · LONDON

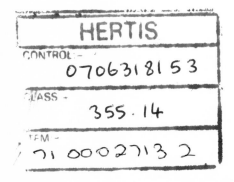

Contents

1 *Frederick II and the Prussian army*

"The art of war" said Frederick II, "is like a great game of chance in which he who has the greatest skill will win in the long run."

His father, King Frederick William of Prussia (1713–40), had left him a superbly equipped and trained army. This despotic monarch, nicknamed the "Sergeant-King", originated the world-famous and unique Prussian discipline. The troops had to drill in perfect time, and to undergo endless "manual exercises" (arms drill), which the King considered the most pleasing form of military exercise. It was too bad for the awkward men, on whom punishments were rained. One such punishment was "running the gauntlet", when the offender had to run stripped to the buff, between the ranks of his fellows who lashed him with their ram-rods[1].

At the beginning of his reign, King Frederick I had to replace the losses incurred in the war against France. The recruiters used the worst possible methods to get suitable young men, going even to the extent of enrolling children only seven years old in the reserve! The result of such practices soon made itself felt. Young men left their homeland in hordes, deserting the fields and workshops. The "Sergeant-King" realised his mistake and introduced two years' compulsory military service, which restored the confidence of the young Prussians who were happy to return to their families.

All the same, it soon became obvious that this system could not provide sufficient numbers, so the recruiters tried their hand abroad. One recruit caught in this way was a young Frenchman who enlisted as a grenadier in the service of the King of Prussia, and later became Marshal of the Empire (under Napoleon I)–his name was Augereau[2].

As the King of Prussia lay dying, he ordered his splendid bodyguard to march past the foot of his bed. They were all giants, and his love of their uniform was such that the mere sight of these resplendent soldiers consoled him in his agony.

This extraordinary man's heir, Crown Prince Frederick, was small and slender, and his father had always regarded him as the perfect good-for-nothing. From the age of four, Frederick was initiated into the finer points of the Prussian arms-drill, to fencing and horsemanship, although his heart was in classical studies.

It was this young prince, although so different from his father, who was to carry on stage by stage the work begun by the old king.

Having inherited an army reputed to be the best in the world, Frederick II of Prussia (Frederick the Great, 1740–86) was impatient to put it to the test, and the occasion was not long delayed. The death of the Emperor Charles VI of Austria presented the Elector of Bavaria, Charles Albert, with the opportunity to assert his claim to the vacant throne,

1 Wooden or metal rods with which the charge was rammed into the barrel
2 Pierre Augereau (1757–1816) took part in the campaigns of the Revolution, of the Consulate and of the Empire, distinguishing himself at Iena, Eylau, in Spain, and at Leipzig.

UNIFORMS OF THE TIME OF FREDERIC II

1 Prussian Brown Hussar
2 Saxon Cuirassier
3 Walloon Dragoon in the Austrian service (1778)
4 Walloon Grenadier in the Austrian service (1778)
5 Trumpeter, Prussian cuirassiers
6 Württemberg Hussar
7, 8 Prussian Infantry
9 Prussian Fusilier
10 Prussian Grenadier of the Guard

with the backing of his French allies. However, the late Emperor's will contained a clause to the effect that the claims of the Elector of Bavaria should not take effect unless the house of Hapsburg had become extinct. The crown thus passed to Maria Theresa, his eldest daughter.

Frederick II decided that the moment had come for action. The philosopher turned wolf; on 16 December 1740 he invaded Silesia, offering Maria Theresa the help of the Prussian army in return for the territory which he had just taken from her.

But, far from being the rather odd young woman everyone thought her, Maria Theresa coped with the situation with astounding energy. So began the war of the Austrian Succession.

Frederick had an easy victory in Silesia, for the Austrian army, exhausted by a succession of wars, was short of troops, funds, and ammunition. But by the spring of 1741, Maria Theresa had established a reliable army, and furthermore she took up the offensive.

Unfortunately, her Commander-in-Chief, General Neipperg, employed the rather cautious methods of the time. Disinclined to risk a pitched battle he manoeuvred his troops interminably, hoping to force the Prussians to retreat by cutting off their rearguard. After eight days spent wallowing in the mud, the much-harassed Austrian army halted in two adjacent villages in the north of Silesia. One of these, Mollwitz[1], was to give its name to a famous battle. Neipperg was unaware that Frederick had forseen the danger and had moved his troops into the area. The opportunity was too good to miss. His fresh troops, attacking on the morning of the 10 April, took the enemy, still suffering from fatigue, completely by surprise. Moreover the Austrian General had left his artillery far to the south. For his part, however, Frederick had not made the same mistake, and his artillery pounded the Austrians along the entire front.

The first to make a move were the cavalry on the Austrian left wing. The deadly fire of the Prussians made them lose their heads, and they charged the enemy cavalry regardlessly and with such fury that the Prussian cavalry were completely routed. Frederick himself fled shamefully down the road to Breslau, but this did not prevent him from treating his cavalry to sarcastic comments about giants on elephants, equally incapable of manoeuvring and fighting, slow and ineffective.

Fortunately for the King of Prussia, Field-Marshal Count Schwerin[2] did not lose his head. He took command of the infantry which, thanks to its excellent discipline, had quickly reformed its ranks, and counter-attacked in perfect order. This remarkable recovery demoralised the Austrians who, unaccustomed to war, at once retreated. Defeat was turned into victory. Frederick must have been profoundly mortified when he realised that he had left to another the glory of an easy triumph. He would never forget it!

1 Malujowice, in Poland
2 Christopher von Schwerin (1684–1757), killed in the siege of Prague

BRITISH INFANTRY IN THE SECOND HALF OF THE 18TH CENTURY

1 Marine, London Volunteer Corps (1799)
2 Private, 2nd Foot Guards (1789)
3 Infantry of the Line (1760)
4 Officer, Foot Guards (1775)
5 Bethnal Green Volunteers (1799)
6 Sergeant-Major, Infantry of the Line
7 Private, 42nd Highland Regiment (1751)
8 Private, Royal Fusiliers (1789)

1

2

3

4

5

6

7

8

This victory was not only the first military defeat of the young Maria Theresa of Austria, but, what was infinitely more serious, it was a signal for a general rush for the spoils. France, Bavaria and Spain, unwilling to see the King of Prussia enrich himself so easily, entered into the competition. The Franco-Bavarian army invaded upper Austria and Bohemia, the Spanish marched into Italy, and Frederick, left behind, occupied Moravia.

Just when all seemed lost, Maria Theresa managed to awake in her Hungarian subjects, despite their uncertain allegiance, a feeling of loyalty. On 1 January 1742, the Austrian army attacked in Bavaria, and Munich surrendered on 14 February. But she was less fortunate at Chotusitz[1] in May, when Frederick gained the upper hand and forced her to give up Silesia. On the credit side, Saxony had withdrawn from the war, and Prussia was pre-occupied by the Dutch, British-Hanoverian and Austrian coalition.

Maria Theresa was soon in a position to re-conquer Silesia. Frederick appreciated this and hastened to conclude a new alliance with France, whereupon he invaded Bohemia. But this time, fate did not smile on him; Duke Charles of Lorraine forced him into an inglorious retreat, which resulted in the ruin of his reputation as a military leader. Naturally his French ally abandoned him, preferring to seek glory in Belgium. An army commanded by Maurice of Saxony[2] was sent to the assistance of the forces besieging Tournai who were threatened by the Dutch and the Anglo-Hanoverians.

Marshal Saxe established his army, some 40,000 strong, astride Antoing-Fontenoy-Bois-de-Barry, drawn up in four lines with a hundred pieces of artillery distributed along its front. At five o'clock in the morning on 11 May 1745, the battle began with the traditional exchange of artillery fire, after which the 53,000-strong army under the British general, the Duke of Cumberland[3], advanced towards the French lines.

The Dutch attacked from the south, and the British-Hanoverians in the centre. Only the latter, forming the principal mass, managed to gain any initial advantage. Then followed the celebrated exchange of the courteous civilities: "Your turn to fire, you Frenchmen," made by Lord Charles Hay, and Auteroche's reply: "No, Sir, please accept the honour . . .", which cost the French dear.

The more usual version is:
Lord Charles Hay: "*Faites tirer vos gens*" ("Order your men to fire.") Auteroche: "*Non, monsieur, à vous l'honneur.*" ("No, sir, you shall have the honour.")

1 Chotusice, in Czechoslovakia
2 Maurice of Saxony, known as Marshal Saxe (1696–1750), entered the service of France in 1720 and devoted all his energies to the War of the Austrian Succession. Louis XV granted him the Château of Chambord.
3 William, Duke of Cumberland (1721–1765), third son of King George II

BRITISH AND HANOVERIAN CAVALRY IN THE LATE 18TH CENTURY

1 Private, 2nd Horse (1751)
2 Soldier, 3rd Horse, Hanover (1758)
3 Carabinier, Hanover (1758)
4 Luckner Hussar, Hanover (1759)
5 17th Light Dragoons (1759)
6 Private, Royal Horse Guards (1798)
7 Kettledrummer, 2nd Horse (1751)
8 Officer, 7th Queen's Own Light Dragoons (1798)
9 Light Cavalryman, Regiment "Frietag" Hanover (1759)

It was two o'clock in the afternoon when the Anglo-Hanoverians, in three attacking columns, came in contact with the first line of the French army and continued to advance in close order resisting all counter-attacks made by the French. The village of Fontenoy was threatened.

It was at this point that a captain in the Regiment of Touraine took the initiative and brought artillery fire to bear on the English column which had closed up forming a compact mass. In a few minutes, the course of the battle was changed. A final charge by the French cavalry routed Cumberland's army.

This magnificent victory did not, however, blind Marshal Saxe to the realities. Making all allowance for the shortcomings of the French infantry in defence in open country, he made it a rule henceforward always to attack first, keeping a large body of troops available so that it could be thrown into battle at a decisive moment.

After Fontenoy, the famous strategist remarked to the King: "You see now what battles are all about."

The resounding victory of Fontenoy was to have repercussions as decisive as they were unexpected on Frederick II who now found himself faced with the alternatives either of winning all along the line or of passing into oblivion along with his little kingdom. Marshal Saxe's success did much to restore his confidence. He decided that a victory over the Austrians would have the effect of restoring his reputation. To this end, he withdrew from the passes leading into Bohemia in order to lure the enemy into Silesia. The Austrians fell into this trap and, on 4 June 1745, appeared before Hohenfrieburg[1], in full view of the Prussian encampment, little thinking that the tents were empty. Under cover of darkness, Frederick had deployed his troops with skill. At about midnight he attacked, and crushed the bewildered Austro-Bavarians with his superior Prussian troops.

The King of Prussia had brought off a spectacular victory, but Maria Theresa was not yet ready to give up. Frederick watched his position become more serious; his soldiers were beginning to desert at an alarming rate. What was worse, his overtures for an armistice were rejected with disdain. Only the British, who were preoccupied with the steady progress of Maurice of Saxony and with the troubles in Scotland, signed a preliminary peace treaty with Prussia.

Frederick turned next against Saxony, the long-standing ally of Austria, defeated the allies at the battle of Kesselsdorf[2], and marched in triumph into Dresden. For the first time his own people called him Frederick the Great. Maria-Theresa was forced by the Treaty of Dresden to abandon Silesia.

But the daughter of Charles VI had not given up yet. At the instigation of her minister Kaunitz, she switched her alliances so that she might crush her detested enemy. France, Russia and Austria united could bring about the dismemberment of

1 Dabromierz, in Poland
2 Near Dresden in east Germany

LOUIS XVI'S CAVALRY
1 Officer, Cuirassiers du Roi (1788)
2 Colonel-General of Hussars (1780)
3 Trumpeter, Mestre-de-camp-general's Regiment
4 Officer, Conti-Dragoons (1786)
5 Carabinier (1787)
6 Artois Dragoons (1788)
7 "Royal Cravatte" Regiment (1786)
8 Cuirassier du Roi (1772)
9 Officer, Bercheny Hussars

Prussia. When Frederick learnt what was afoot, he decided to seize the initiative.

At dawn on 28 August 1756, the King of Prussia marched out of Potsdam at the head of his army, and started a practice that persisted up to the time of Kaiser William II and Adolf Hitler, namely that of invading without declaring war.

The Saxons fell back in disorder on their strongly fortified camp at Pirna[1]. On 1 October 1756 the Austrians, hastening to their rescue, met the Prussians near Lobositz[2].

Although at first the battle went against them, a timely bayonet charge turned the tide in Frederick's favour. This victory resulted in Austria, Russia, France, Sweden, and several of the German states forming a coalition against him.

The next encounter took place near Prague. The Prussians advanced at the high port to within fifty paces of the enemy, although they incurred heavy casualties, before opening fire and then going in with the bayonet. The Prussians lost 18,000 killed and the Allies 12,000.

In the meantime another army was advancing by forced marches. Frederick made contact at Kolin[3], but the exhausted Prussian troops fell back in face of the Austro-Saxon cavalry. Frederick charged in vain at the head of forty men of the Regiment "Alt Dessau" in the hope of rallying his forces, but this time he had to admit defeat, and retreat.

Frederick the Great now turned westwards where he was to encounter French troops for the first time. After months of fruitless effort, he forced the enemy to join battle near Rossbach[4] on 5 November 1757. Twenty-one thousand Prussians faced an army of 64,000, of which the French contingent numbered some 24,000 (some authors give the figures as 11,000 Austrians and 32,000 French).

The Allies were on the defensive; Frederick decided that their position was too strong and fell back, a manoeuvre which the enemy took as an attempt to disengage.

The Allies therefore decided to try to outflank the Prussian army, a manoeuvre much favoured at that time.

Frederick, a born strategist, knew how to turn this rash move to his own advantage. He marshalled his army behind the hills of Janus-Hugel, then altered direction and appeared at the head of the allied columns who were taken completely by surprise. Six Prussian battalions were sufficient, with the help of the cavalry, to achieve in the space of one hour a spectacular victory over an enemy vastly superior in numbers, and who escaped destruction only because night fell. This feat cost Frederick, in all, only 156 men.

Prussia had now become the leading German state.

1 Pirna, near Dresden, in east Germany
2 Lovosice, Czechoslovakia
3 Kolin, in Czechoslovakia
4 Rossbach in the Halle district of east Germany

LOUIS XVI'S INFANTRY

1, 2 Infantry of the Line
3 Light Infantry
4 Alsace Regiment
5 Dillon Regiment
6 Drummer, Swiss Guard
7 French Foot Guard
8 Swiss Guard (1780)
9 French Foot Guards
10 Foot Artillery (1780)
11 Foot Artillery (1789)
12 Royal Baviere (1779)
13 Sapper (1786)
14 Marine

Frederick set out with all speed for Silesia which was once more threatened by the Austrians.

The opposing armies met at Leuthen[1] near Breslau on 5 December in the same year. The Prussians concentrated their attack on the enemy's left, and their well-disciplined cavalry held off the Austrian cavalry, so tipping the balance. Thereupon the rest of the army collapsed and fled, leaving 22,000 prisoners to the Prussians.

These two consecutive victories were greeted by the English with wild enthusiasm. Frederick the Great's brother-in-law, Ferdinand of Brunswick, had meanwhile reorganised the English army which, under his auspices had regained its strength. But fate had other things in store for Frederick; von Daun[2] drove him out of Bohemia, and then Frederick, having defeated the Russians at Zorndorf[3], was himself severely trounced at Hochkirch[4] by the tenacious von Daun. At the end of 1758 the English began to have doubts of their idol, but this extraordinary monarch would not admit defeat. He took the offensive and, at Kunersdorf[5] on 12 August 1759, attacked 50,000 Russians and 30,000 Austrians with his army of 48,000. Some hours later the Prussians numbered only 3,000. Fortunately for Frederick his adversaries did not take full advantage of their victory mainly because of disputes among themselves as to who was to pursue the Prussian army.

The King of Prussia was able to rally to his cause many more men that he had expected. The 3,000 who remained of his army were swollen by more than 20,000 men returning to the colours. All was not lost. In 1760 he defeated the allies at Liegnitz[6] and at Torgau[7], but a year later Pomerania and Silesia fell once more into the hands of the enemy. An unexpected event saved Prussia, namely the death of the Empress of Russia, whose successor, Peter III, was a fervent admirer of Frederick and lost no time in withdrawing the Russian forces from the territories of his hero.

Once peace with Russia was concluded, Sweden also made peace, and shortly afterwards Saxony followed suit. At last, on 15 February 1763, Prussia and Austria signed the peace treaty which put an end to the cruel and utterly pointless conflict, and the parties retained the possessions with which they had started.

Nevertheless, in the eyes of the world, Frederick II became the man of his time and the "marvel" of the 18th century. "Der Alte Fritz", as his people called him, died on 17 August 1786 after a reign of nearly fifty years.

1 Leuthen, near Breslau in Poland
2 Leopold von Daun (1705–1766), defeated at Leuthen, victorious at Kolin and Hofkirchen
3 Sarbinowo, in Poland
4 Hofkirchen, in the Dresden district of East Germany
5 Kunowice, in Poland
6 Legnica, in Poland
7 Torgau, in the Leipzig district of East Germany

SOLDIERS IN THE LATE 18TH CENTURY

1 Royal Liegeois (1788)
2 Swedish Infantry (1779)
3, 4 Walloon Regiment in the Austrian service (1792)
5 Russian Grenadier (1762)
6 Dutch Grenadier (1785)
7 Flanders Regiment of the Army of the Patriots (1789)

8 Brabantine volunteer in the Army of the Patriots (1789)
9 Infantry musket (1760)
10 Prussian musket
11 Cavalry Carbine (1790)
12 English Sharpe pistol
13 Cavalry pistol (1790)
14 French Charleville pistol (1777)

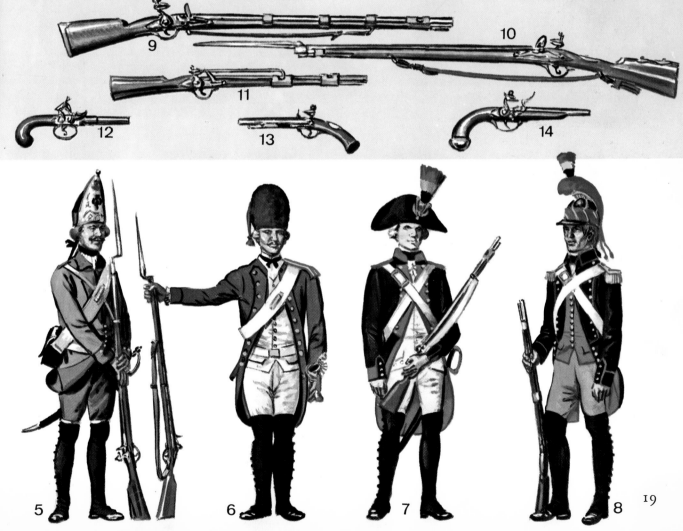

19

2 "Red Coats" and "Rebels"

In 1767, the English minister, Charles Townshend, devised a method of procuring for the Crown an additional revenue of £10,000 a year by levying import duty on tea, glass and paper brought into America. The project was approved almost unanimously by Parliament because the Seven Years' War and the conquest of Canada had proved very costly.

The American colonials–those "sons of liberty", truly a name given ahead of time–reacted violently against this arbitrary measure on the part of London. A scuffle broke out in Boston on 3 March 1770. This was started by several snowballs thrown at the Redcoats by some children, but it degenerated into a brawl and left four Americans on the ground. The hot-heads called this the "Boston Massacre", and the tension mounted until, on 6 December 1773, in Boston again, some troublemakers threw an English cargo of 343 chests of tea into the sea. This outrage against His Majesty's flag was quickly punished. The port was closed and the town was occupied by British soldiers. King George III was firmly of the opinion that the army must be used to keep the restless colonials under the control of the mother country. Boston, however, refused to submit, and soon the other colonies took her side. George Washington took command of the insurgent army, which presented a strange sight with peasants and townsfolk alike dressed and armed in whatever they had. Washington blockaded Boston, and to his great surprise the British surrendered. The insurgents' triumph was short-lived, for England soon sent reinforcements to the American continent, an army of first-class soldiers with the support of a powerful navy. From now on, Washington had to fall back, suffering defeat after defeat. The Northern and Southern States soon found themselves separated from each other by the British columns. Furthermore, troops were sent from Canada in support. The insurgents' position was becoming desperate when, on 17 October 1777, the army from Canada unexpectedly surrendered at Saratoga.

The news of the victory galvanised the Americans and marked the turning point of the War of Independence. This capitulation, which only involved 3,5000 British soldiers still fit for service, had repercussions for the Crown, more serious than the loss of hundreds of thousands of men.

General Burgoyne's army set off for Lake Champlain; it numbered 3,700 English, 3,000 Germans, 500 Indians, who along with the artillery, the Canadians and a few American loyalists, made up a force of around 8,000 men.

Was it mediocrity which was responsible for the sad end of this army? Quite the contrary: it was made up of excellent troops and led by men of exceptional ability.

Twenty days after his departure, Burgoyne had stormed the great fort of Ticonderoga and had advanced 200 kilometres, capturing 128 guns and numerous prisoners with the loss of only 200 men. It was at this stage that his difficulties began. In his hopes to join Howe's forces near Albany, Burgoyne set off through the forests and broken country separating him from his goal, and Washington knew how to take advantage of this move. The insurgents blocked the roads by felling all the biggest trees along the way and laid waste the countryside. The progress of the British force became extremely slow and difficult.

Two detachments in succession sent by Burgoyne to procure horses and cattle were destroyed by the American Militia and the Green Mountains Boys lying in ambush.

WAR OF AMERICAN INDEPENDENCE (I)

1, 3, 5, 6 American militia
2 American Infantry (1781)
4 American Dragoon
7 Fusilier, Regiment Royal Auvergne (France)
8 Fusilier, Regiment Royal Deux-Ponts (France)
9 French Hussar
10 Fusilier, Dillon Regiment (France)
11 Gunner, Lauzun Brigade (France)

On top of everything else, Burgoyne did not know that the man he was trying to join at Albany had left several weeks before to lay siege to Philadelphia. The ill-starred general set off for Saratoga and encountered an American army of 14,000 holding strong positions on the Bemis Heights. Dividing his 5,000 men into three columns, he attacked.

The combat was particularly bitter, especially in the centre, where an American officer, Benedict Arnold, performed prodigious feats of valour with his militia. The British ended the day as masters of the field, but they had lost 600 men, including many officers, killed by the American marksmen.

The news of the imminent arrival of a relieving army from New York instilled some hope into the British General, but the insurgents, who were watching the roads, cut off the reinforcements. On 7 October, Burgoyne attempted a fresh attack but this was repulsed with heavy casualties. The autumn rains had started. Half-dead with hunger, the British tried to fall back on Lake Champlain, but it was too late: they were forced to surrender, and the only concession granted was that they should march out with the honours of war, and be allowed safe conduct to Great Britain. On their final parade, the British and Hessian Regiments burnt their colours.

News of this victory had only just arrived when France, an absolute monarchy, declared for the American republicans who were ably represented in Paris by Benjamin Franklin. The treaty of alliance was signed on 6 February 1778, while most of the countries of Europe were praying for the defeat of England.

The first experiences of the French expeditionary force were not particularly happy ones: La Fayette was beaten by Cornwallis on the way to Yorktown in Virginia.

Meanwhile, Washington and Rochambeau hastened to join La Fayette, bringing with them 9,000 Americans who had been trained by Baron von Steuben, 7,000 French troops, and 92 pieces of artillery. The siege of Yorktown began on 6 October 1781. The bombardment was opened by Washington himself three days later, and, continuing incessantly, worsened every day, so that Cornwallis, who was short of ammunition, could only put up a weak resistance.

On 14 October, under cover of darkness, two parties, one American and the other French, each launched an attack on a redoubt in the defences of Yorktown. The clash was violent, and the Americans had reason to be grateful for the thorough training that von Stueben had given them in close combat. On their side, the French of the Gatinais Regiment took their objective with the greatest ease. An heroic attempt by the British to retake the redoubts was repulsed with heavy losses several days later. Cornwallis was thus forced to surrender on 19 October 1781. Magnificent in their uniforms, the British and German troops marched past their conquerors to the sound of fifes and drums, heads held high and hate in their hearts. This was the end, although the hostilities in fact dragged on uselessly for another two years. Thus the Republic of the United States of America was born.

WAR OF AMERICAN INDEPENDENCE (II)

1 Private, Black Watch, British Army
2 Private, Legion Cavalry
3 Officer, Grenadier Company, British Army
4 Ranger
5 German foot soldier
6 German dragoon
7 Anspach-Bayreuth Regiment (German)
8 Anhalt-Zerbst Regiment (German)
9 Hessian musket
10 Belgian pistol
11 Socket bayonet
12 Hessian grenadier's musket
13 British "Brown Bess"
14 North and Cheney pistol (1799)
15 British cavalry pistol

The military tactics of Frederick II of Prussia had plunged foreign strategists into perplexity. A famous argument developed between the exponents of the "order mince" and those of the "ordre profond". Was it better to attack in extended order which allowed a greater fire power along the front, or to attack in columns in close order?

The Frenchman, Guibert,[1] tried combining the two by placing his columns so that they could redeploy rapidly and thus provide increased fire power. At the end of the reign of Louis XVI, this solution was adopted and was followed during the Republic and the Empire.

From this time, recruiting became more selective. Boys were enlisted from the age of sixteen, or younger in the case of the sons of "military families". These young recruits spent the first years of their service as trumpeters or as drummers. Tall youths of good appearance were much in demand and the recruiting posters often set out these particulars, emphasising the many advantages of becoming a soldier and describing, down to the last detail, the splendid uniform that he would have the joy of wearing. The soldier ceased to be a mere adventurer and became conscious of the esprit-de-corps special to each arm of the service, with its traditions and marches.

Training had advanced considerably, and each regiment made it a point of honour to try to appear to the best advantage at parades and reviews.

The Royal Household had its own regiments; the Swiss Guards dressed in red, the Body Guard, and the Foot Guards.

Rifle Regiments were introduced at the end of the reign of Louis XVI to meet the urgent need for light troops.

The artillery had already known in the reign of Louis XV the beginnings of reform under the influence of Gribeauval,[2] a French lieutenant-colonel, who had served under the Austrians and achieved the rank of field-marshal. Later he returned to the French service under Louis XVI, where his work consisted for the most part in organising the artillery in four classes: field, siege, garrison and coast.

Field artillery was made lighter and more solid. In the long term, the most important change was the introduction of three calibres: 12, 8 and 4 inches, and howitzers of 8 and 4 inches. The guns had a range of 1,500 metres and became more accurate after Gribeauval had devised an adjustable back-sight operated by a screw which enabled the elevation to be adjusted according to the range. This military genius also invented the "prolonge" which made it possible to move the gun while unlimbered.

At the same time, another great power, Great Britain, produced an army run on very different lines. The discipline here was much more rude and rigid, and all misdemeanors were punished with

1 Francois de Guibert (1744–1790) was the author of *Essai de la tactique generale* and *Defense du système de la guerre moderne.* His theories had some part in Napoleon's military thinking.
2 Jean-Baptiste de Gribeauval (1715–1789); his artillery played an important part in the campaigns of the Revolution and the Empire

THE FRENCH REVOLUTION (I)

1 Rifleman
2 Infantry of the Line
3 Belgian volunteer
4 Dragoon
5 Grenadier
6 Cuirassier
7 Hussar
8 Gendarme
9 Light cavalry
10 Artillery
11 Hussar of the Escort
12 General Officer
13 People's Commissary with the armies
14 Observation balloon

extreme severity. The lash was frequently used, sometimes 1,500 strokes . . . fortunately spread over more than one session.

The Tower musket weighing 15 pounds was splendidly maintained; each soldier carried with him the necessary spare parts for its perfect performance. Its range was comparatively short, and its accuracy doubtful at more than about 40 metres. The experience of the War of Independence showed that the muskets of the insurgents had a longer range and were more accurate, but had the disadvantage of taking longer to load and reload.

The discomfort of the barracks and the poor quality of the food led the officers and men alike to look outside for more acceptable lodgings, and, as with most regiments stationed for many years in one place, many of the men practised another career, or managed a small farm. This system lasted up to 1881, when a system of regular reliefs was introduced, so that regiments served in rotation in all parts of the Empire.

Despite the hard life, the British soldier soon regained the "old spirit" and did not forfeit his reputation for gallantry and tenacity, and he showed it again and again in the course of the century, notably during the siege of Gibraltar by the French and the Spanish. Between 1779 and 1783, the men of the Royal Sappers and Miners, although mainly concerned in defending their position, were still able to dig most of the galleries and casemates existing on the Rock to this day.

The experience of the war against France in Canada in 1754 gave birth to the light infantry, made up of agile and intelligent soldiers. Their equipment was lightened, and their training based on that of the American Rangers. This practice was adopted by all infantry regiments, which henceforth always included a light infantry company.

At the beginning of the 19th century the British soldier still carried the old "Brown Bess" introduced in about 1690. This weapon had an effective range of less than 100 metres, and was very inaccurate. At the same time, despite these defects, the "Brown Bess", as history has shown, was adequate for firing volleys which then played an important part in warfare. This weapon got its name from the colour of the barrel, which was "browned" with acid. In 1759 a new type of cavalry – the light dragoon – was introduced, and they quickly proved their value as flank guards. Furthermore, their mobility allowed them to be moved rapidly to any place where they might be required.

The artillery, however, lacked mobility. It was drawn by heavy draught horses with dismounted civilian drivers. In 1793 innovations were made, and light artillery that could keep up with the cavalry was introduced. Because of its speed of movement these became known as "Galloper Guns" and "Flying Artillery".

With the advent of the Horse Artillery (to give it the proper title) in England, a horse-drawn vehicle (known as the "Military Fly") was devised for the rapid transport of infantry (thirty men seated back to back), but this remarkable machine never saw service.

During this time, movements were starting in France that would shake all Europe. The British were not greatly surprised at this. After all, the French, who were eccentrics anyway, were quite at liberty to throw off the yoke of absolute monarchy. The kings of Europe however smelt danger; France suddenly found 90,000 Austrians and Prussians under the Duke of Brunswick descending upon her. The attack was halted at Valmy on 20 September 1792 and beaten back at Jemmapes[1] on 6 November. Belgium was annexed by France.

1 Jemappes, in the Hainaut province of Belgium

THE FRENCH REVOLUTION (II)
1 Carabinier (1793)
2 Light Infantry (1793)
3 Dragoon (1795)
4 Fusilier (1791)
5 Infantry (1793)
6 Carabinier (1792)
7 Hussar
8 Grenadier (1791)
9 Cavalry (1792)
10 Light Cavalry (1791)
11 Cavalry (1792)
12 Carabinier (1792)
13 Gunner (1792)

On 1 February 1793 the Convention declared war on England, and six weeks later the Austrians drove the French armies out of Belgium; the French commander-in-chief, Dumouriez, found it wiser to take service with the Austrians. In the spring all Europe joined forces against revolutionary France.

France showed the world what the irresistible will of a people defending their homeland could do. Herded together in disorder, the "volunteers" hastily learned how to handle arms under the iron rule of the old uncommissioned officers of the Royal Army, the army that they had scorned and dismembered in their exaggerated revolutionary zeal.

Ill equipped, with bits of string as braces, poorly-shod, and supplementing their forage requisitions by plunder, these men stemmed this avalanche of enemies; they advanced with cries of *Vive la Nation* or "Navarre unafraid", shouting from force of habit war-cries of 200 years earlier.

Their patriotic enthusiasm made up for their shortcomings as tactitians. They launched frontal attacks and their ardour did the rest. But, after Jemmapes they suffered a succession of reverses. There was an uprising in the Vendee, which was royalist.

"Victory or death", the Convention proclaimed. On 24 February 1793 they called up all unmarried men between the ages of 18 and 40; but less than half of the expected 300,000 men reported. Dire penalties were decreed against those who failed to present themselves, and on 23 August general mobilisation was ordered and 435,000 men aged between 18 and 25 were mustered.

Carnot, a former officer of the Engineers in the Royal Army took over the Ministry of War and restored the situation, which earned him the title of "Organisateur de la Victoire". Among his collaborators was a young officer called Napoleon Bonaparte.

On 8 January 1794 the oft-wished-for "amalgamation" was approved by the Convention. This measure brought about the fusion of the army and the ill-disciplined volunteers and they were re-organised in demi-brigades of three battalions. This was put into effect with due solemnity to the strains of the Marseillaise. The 213 line battalions absorbed the 725 battalions of volunteers to form 213 demi-brigades.

The old soldiers, who were still dressed in white, changed into the blue uniform of the volunteers. The nickname "Young Blues", given to the recruits in the French army today, dates from this time.

At this time too, the *Central Commission for the Manufacture of Arms and Gunpowder* considerably improved the supply of arms and ammunition. Those responsible for the national defence availed themselves of the latest scientific developments – Chappe's telegraph and the observation balloon.

Out of the chaos of these first years, Carnot had produced an army which, though not yet perfect, was nevertheless beginning to show signs of efficiency. Jourdan, Hoche, Pichegru, and Bonaparte respectively, were given command of the armies of the North, of the Moselle, of the Rhine, and of Italy.

From now on make-shift was abandoned. The disposition of the enemy was carefully studied; every endeavour was made to use to the best advantage their available forces. Enemies fell back on every side before a nation that put the war first, even to the cobblers who had to deliver five pairs of shoes every ten days. (In 1793 the Republic replaced the week by the "decade".) These shoes had square toes to prevent the soldiers selling them to the civilians.

All that the armies of the Republic now needed to enjoy everlasting fame was a leader, and they found him in General Bonaparte who was then 26 years old.

THE AUSTRIAN ARMY
1 Flemish dragoon in the Army of the Patriots (1789)
2 Regiment of Vierzet (1785)
3 Grenadier in the Regiment of Württemberg (1795)
4 Mounted Police (1793)
5 Dragoon in the Regiment of Namur, Army of the Patriots (1789)
6 Ensign of the Regiment of Clerfayt (1792)
7 Line Regiment (1790)
8 Regiment of the Archduke Joseph (1802)
9 Dragoons of Latour (1790)

In Italy in 1796, Bonaparte crushed the Austrians at Montenotte, Millesimo and Dego, and the Sardinians at Mondovi. The following month saw a victory at Lodi, then at Castiglione on 5 August, and finally at Arcole, where on 15, 16 and 17 November the young general charged at the head of his troops. After a further victory at Rivoli on 14 January 1797, Bonaparte concluded an armistice with the Austrians on 7 April of that year.

There remained England. Bonaparte considered that an invasion of Britain was impossible, and so decided to strike in Egypt to threaten the routes to India.

On 1 July 1789, Napoleon Bonaparte landed part of the army of Italy and the best troops of the army of the Rhine at Alexandria. Among his officers were Lannes, Berthier, Murat, Desaix, and Kleber. In addition the young commander-in-chief took with him a team of experts who laid the foundations of modern Egyptology.

The first action took place on 21 July 1798, when the French defeated the Mamelukes in the Battle of the Pyramids, but on 1 August Nelson destroyed Napoleon's fleet in the harbour at Aboukir. Pushing eastwards, Napoleon destroyed the Turkish force under the Pacha of Damascus on Mount Tabor on 16 April 1799, only to be halted before Saint Jean d'Arce by a British officer.

Having lost 5,000 men, Bonaparte ordered his troops to withdraw. The march was long and arduous, but this did not prevent him from destroying a Turkish landing force at Aboukir on 25 July 1799.

Disillusioned, Bonaparte handed over the army of Egypt to Kleber, and went back to France.

THE EGYPTIAN ARMY
1 Dragoons of Kleber
2 Dromedary Regiment
3 Trumpeter, Dromedary Regiment
4 Hussar
5 Grenadier, Demi-brigade
6 Light infantry
7 Coptic Legion
8, 9 Demi-brigade (1801)

4 *The Napoleonic wars*

The Egyptian expedition had awoken hatred and fear of the French throughout Europe. A new coalition was formed at the instance of William Pitt, the youngest man to hold office as Prime Minister in English history.

The result was soon felt. England, Austria, Russia, Turkey and the Kingdom of Naples took the initiative. No sooner had Bonaparte returned from Egypt than he learned of the loss of Italy where Moreau, Jourdan and Macdonald had been defeated by General Souvarov[1], whose tactical skill equalled that of Napoleon.

It was to General Massena that the honour of saving the Republic fell. He held Switzerland by defeating the Russians under Korsakov[2]. At the same time, Brune drove the British out of Holland. General Bonaparte, whose reputation had suffered little from the Egyptian fiasco, quickly realised that France was being ruined by the ineptitude and cupidity of the Directoire and needed a man who would save her from collapse.

The coup d'etat of 18th Brumaire VIII according to the French Republican Calendar (9 November 1799) placed the State under the rule of three consuls; but in fact, Bonaparte was the sole ruler of France.

The First Consul's prime consideration was to rescue the army from the deplorable state in which it found itself. Its doors were thrown open once more to veterans, pensioners, emigres, and officers of the old regime. He re-equipped the troops, revised the pay system, established a staff corps, and replaced the civilian artillery drivers by an artillery train. At the same time, he reorganised the army into a number of demi-brigades of infantry, a regiment of light cavalry, and some dozen guns, the remainder of the cavalry and artillery forming a mobile reserve. The Consular Guard was organised on the lines of the future Imperial Guard.

Meanwhile, the Army of Egypt was fully occupied. A British force under Abercrombie[3] had disembarked at Aboukir, near Alexandria, the place where Nelson had destroyed Bonaparte's fleet three years before.

The British landing was planned to take place at night, but was delayed until after day-break by the late arrival of several ships at the rendezvous. They came under heavy artillery fire and were attacked by the French cavalry as they came ashore. However, the landing was ultimately successful.

On 21 March 1801, a strong French counter-attack just before night fell developed into the Battle of Alexandria. The British 28th Foot, who were in the Reserve Brigade and occupying some partially constructed defences in the area of a ruined palace, were surrounded by columns of the French 'Invincible Legion', but they beat off the attack despite

1 Alexander Vassilievitch Souvarov, or Souvorov (1729–1800), who had campaigned in Poland and brought victories against the Turks, was put at the head of the armies entrusted with the task of driving the French out of Italy.
2 Alexander Mikhailovitch Korsakov (1753–1840)
3 Sir Ralph Abercrombie (1734–1801) fought the French in Holland, the West Indies and in Egypt

FRENCH ARMY UNDER THE CONSULATE AND THE EMPIRE
1 Officer, Horse Grenadiers (1803)
2 Carabinier (1801)
3 Horse Artillery
4 Sergeant of Grenadiers, Consular Guard (1802)
5 Foot Artillery (1801)
6 Military Mounted Police (1802)

33

the enemy's superiority in numbers. Their heroic resistance saved the British army from defeat. The French launched a vigorous cavalry charge supported by infantry, which was broken by the main body of the army. The British lost their Commander-in-Chief, 70 officers and 1,306 men, and the French 3,000.

In this action, the 28th Foot (now the Gloucestershire Regiment) fought back to back, and this is commemorated to this day by the Regiment's wearing a 'Back Badge', a small badge, now in the form of the 'Sphinx and Egypt' within a wreath, that is worn on the back of the head-dress.

After this battle, the abandoned French army was involved only in sporadic fighting and was forced to surrender. The British regiments that fought in the campaign were awarded the badge of the Sphinx superseded Egypt, which was borne on their standards and columns.

At this time, Europe was not much concerned with the happenings in Egypt. In Germany, General Moreau, to whom Bonaparte had entrusted 120,000 of his best troops along with Ney and Grouchy, had won victories at Biberach,[1] Höchstädt and Hohenlinden[2] though he took longer about it than Bonaparte would have wished.

In Italy, Massena had retreated before an army of 80,000 under von Melas.[3]

For Bonaparte the time had come to intervene personally. At the head of the Army of Reserve, he crossed the St Bernard Pass between 15 and 20 May in the face of considerable difficulties. On 9 June the French advance guard under Lannes defeated the Austrian army which had just forced Massena to surrender Genoa. On 14 June, Bonaparte met

Melas and the Austrian army at Marengo. At three o'clock in the afternoon, his troops started to fall back under heavy fire. Suddenly, at about seven o'clock in the evening, Desaix arrived and saved the day, but was himself killed leading the Boudet[4] division.

Bonaparte took all the credit, and his personal prestige was greatly enhanced.

The peace treaty was signed at Luneville in 1801, and in 1802 the First Consul took it upon himself to organise the army according to his own ideas—the Grand Army was born.

In 1801 the army was in very poor state. Successive campaigns had taken their toll of uniforms and arms, and there was a shortage of horses.

The Treaty of Amiens, concluded with England in March 1802, gave France an opportunity to put new life into her declining industry.

On 2 August 1802, Napoleon Bonaparte was elected Consul for life. On 2 December 1804 he had himself crowned Emperor of the French at Notre-Dame in Paris, and, on the following day on the Champ-de-Mars, his regiments received their new standards—Imperial Eagles.

In 1805, Bonaparte had an army of about 450,000 infantry, composed of 90 line regiments and 26 light infantry regiments. The infantry were armed with flintlock muskets and bayonets inherited from the former army, and with small, slightly curved

1 In the Bade Wurttemberg district, in East Germany
2 In Bavaria
3 Michael von Melas (1729–1806), who was defeated at Marengo
4 The victory of Essling (1809) was also due to this division

THE FRENCH ARMY UNDER THE EMPIRE (I)

1 Engineers, Imperial Guard
2 Corporal, Light Infantry (1804)
3 "Pupille", Imperial Guard
4 Grenadier, Imperial Guard
5 Military Foot Police (*Gendarme d'elite a pied*), Imperial Guard
6 Light Infantry, Regiment of the Line (1807)
7 Light Infantryman in winter uniform
8 Private, Fusiliers
9 l'Ecole Polytechnique (1809)
10 Drummer, Fusiliers (1807)

swords called 'briquets'. 80,000 strong, the cavalry was divided into the heavy cavalry (cuirassiers), cavalry of the line (dragoons and lancers), and light cavalry (chasseurs and hussars).

The artillery, which was still the same as in the days of Gribeauval, had an effective strength of 30,000 men at the beginning of Napoleon's reign, but doubled this figure within a few years. It was divided into companies of 120 men and eight guns, with a range of 3,000 metres and firing two rounds a minute.

The Consular Guard was replaced by the Imperial Guard, 8,000 strong, including 5,000 infantry, 2,000 cavalry, and 24 guns. It was made up of former non-commissioned officers and selected men with not less than six years' service. The best-looking and tallest men served in the Grenadiers, and to prevent jealousy the less tall went to the light infantry. The private soldiers held the rank of Sergeant, the Corporals that of Sergeant-Major, and the Sergeant-Majors that of Second Lieutenant.

This Corps, which was to become more famous than all the rest, had increased to 25,000 men by 1809, and by 1812 had assumed the proportions of a separate army.

The peace came to an end in 1803; Napoleon massed the Grand Army around Boulogne attempting to repeat the exploits of William the Conqueror. He built a fleet of flat-bottomed barges, which caused panic across the Channel and encouraged enrolment in the Volunteers. But in the autumn of 1805, Napoleon suddenly struck his tents and, led by their Eagles, the Grand Army set off by forced marches eastwards for Vienna.

Britain owed this sudden change of plan to the vigilance of the Royal Navy, and to the unsea-worthiness of Napoleon's barges.

The Grand Army was for the first time divided into seven corps, each under a Marshal. Napoleon had under his command eighteen Marshals, aged from 34 to 51: Augereau, Bernadotte, Berthier, Bessieres, Brune, Davout, Jourdan, Kellermann, Lannes, Lefebvre, Massena, Moncey, Mortier, Murat, Ney, Perignon, Serurier, and Soult.

The average age of the colonels was 39, and that of the generals 29. It was men like these, young and enthusiastic, backed by experienced non-commissioned officers and hardy troops, all thirsting for glory, that would bring Europe to her knees before the Emperor.

Each army corps had a strength of 25–30,000 men, with headquarter staff, two or three infantry divisions, a light cavalry division, its own artillery, and a transport train. Furthermore, the Emperor also had at his disposal a general cavalry reserve consisting of cuirassiers, carabiniers, dragoons, hussars and chasseurs, which, with light artillery, formed the *Avant-Garde generale*, placed under the command of a proven leader.

Finally, there was an artillery reserve formed of regiments of 50, 100 and 150 guns, with a total strength in 1805 of 21,950 pieces, and this was augmented later on.

Like a torrent, the Grand Army spread out towards the Rhine and trapped the 40,000 Austrians under von Mack,[1] who, realising the position too late,

1 Karl von Mack (1752–1828)

THE FRENCH ARMY UNDER THE EMPIRE (II)

1 Dragoon, Regiment of the Empress (1802–1814)
2 Cuirassier (1812)
3 Lancer, Imperial Guard
4 Carabinier (1812)
5 Horse grenadier, Imperial Guard
6 Light cavalryman, Imperial Guard
7 Mameluke, Imperial Guard
8 Polish lancer, Imperial Guard

tried to get away, only to come up against the Emperor's armies at Wertingen, Memmingen, and Elchingen[1]. He took refuge in Ulm, and on 13 October 1805 surrendered with the 25,000 men still remaining.

This series of victories, won over a period of less than a fortnight led to a saying among the men: "It is not with our arms, but with our legs that the Emperor defeats the Austrians."

The Russians, under the one-eyed General Koutousov[2], were approaching, so Napoleon sent the *Avant-Garde generale* to intercept them. The Russians chose to fall back and, crossing the Danube, rejoined Buxhovden's[3] reinforcements at Olmütz[4].

On 13 November, Napoleon entered Vienna and, on 2 December, joined battle with the Austrian and Russian forces between Pratzen and Austerlitz.[5]

On the eve of the battle, looking at the enemy, Napoleon said: "Before tomorrow night comes, that army will be in my hands."

At the battle of Austerlitz, also called the battle of the three Emperors (Napoleon, Francis II of Austria, and Alexander I of Russia), 105,000 Austrians and Russians opposed 60,000 French. In less than an hour, the left flank of the Allies had been broken, and by one o'clock in the afternoon thousands of Russians had drowned in the freezing ponds. Victory was complete. In the light of the pale sun, 30,000 prisoners filed past, and their richly decorated standards were stacked in great piles. The guns taken from the enemy were melted down to make the great column which was erected to the honour of the Grand Army in the *Place Vendome* in Paris.

Napoleon could now say to his soldiers: "You have now covered your Eagles with an immortal glory. It will be enough that you say, 'I was at Austerlitz' for all who hear to reply, 'There goes a brave man.'"

Peace was signed on 27 December, and this time it seemed likely that it would last, for now even Britain seemed anxious to come to terms with the Ogre.

In Britain, Charles James Fox had succeeded Pitt as Foreign Minister and, being of the opinion that war was incompatible with civilisation, he had great hopes that the peace would last. However, his efforts were in vain "Europe is on the brink of an abyss," he said. Unfortunately death thwarted his attempts at reconciliation, and hostilities broke out again.

This time it was Prussia, now under Frederick William III, the unworthy successor to 'Old Fritz'; and Russia now in alliance with Britain, that combined together against Napoleon. He moved immediately with the aim of crushing the Prussians before the Russians arrived.

The Prussian army held no secrets for Napoleon, who understood its system of manoeuvre, and was well aware of the strength of its cavalry and the excellence of its artillery. But Frederick William III's commanders were tired, hide-bound old men,

1 In Bavaria. Marshal Ney received the title of Duke of Elchingen
2 Mikhail Illarionovitch Golenichtchev Koutousov [Koutouzov], 1745–1813. Napoleon fought against him again at Moscow and in the retreat
3 Frederic de Buxhovden (1750–1811) commanded the Russians at Austerlitz
4 Olomouc, in Czechoslovakia
5 Slavkov, in Czechoslovakia

THE FRENCH ARMY UNDER THE EMPIRE (III)

1 Military Mounted Police
2 Trumpeter, Lancers, Imperial Guard
3 Conscript, Rifles, Imperial Guard
4 Light infantry, Imperial Guard
5 Garde d'honneur
6 Artillery Train, and Train of the Imperial Guard
7 Scout, Old Guard

still faithful to the outdated theories of Frederick the Great.

At the end of September 1806, 175,000 Prussians appeared between Eisenach and Jena[1] on a front of 100 kilometres. Deciding to take the offensive, the Prussians directed the main body of their army of 125,000 men towards the Main in order to cut the French lines of communication while Hohenlohe[2] set off with 50,000 men to intercept them.

Meanwhile, Napoleon had secretly turned his forces towards Saxony, and soon Hohenlohe came up against Murat who forced him to retreat. Lannes, for his part, defeated Prince Ludwig of Prussia at Saalfeld. The main body of the Prussian army at once fell back on Magdeburg and Berlin, but it was already too late. Napoleon cut off their retreat which involved them in two battles: one at Auerstadt [3], and the other, where the Emperor commanded in person, at Jena.

The Battle of Jena opened on 14 October, under a clear autumn sky. Some hours later the Prussian army had been totally defeated. The Prussians lost 20,000 killed and wounded and 40,000 prisoners including 20 generals, as well as about 30 standards and 300 guns.

During the battle, one grenadier of the Guard, impatient to fight, had cried out: "*En avant!*" (Forward!), and Napoleon, who never let an opportunity pass of bolstering up his image, replied: "What is this? Only a beardless young man would dare to tell me what I should do. Let him wait until he has commanded in as many pitched battles as I have before he presumes to give me advice ..."

To add to this spectacular victory, which marked the apogee of Napoleonic glory, 14,000 prisoners and 100 guns were taken at the capitulation of Erfurt. After Napoleon's entry into Berlin on 27 October, the King of Prussia had only 15,000 men left; his army had collapsed like a house of cards.

But Britain and Russia had not yet given up the struggle. Determined to finish off his old enemy, Napoleon established the continental blockade, an overrated idea that had little effect on the subjects of King George III. In the case of the Russians, he set about attacking them in Poland where the Grand Army and its allies had their taste of the winter.

When he arrived at Warsaw on the heels of Murat on 19 December 1807, Napoleon found 60,000 Russians on the Narav awaiting reinforcements. Napoleon crossed the Vistula and defeated the Russians at Kzarnowo, Pultusk, Golymin and Soldau[4]. Winter was drawing on, and it grew colder and colder; the Grand Army would have happily stayed where they were until spring. The Russian General Bennigsen[5] and his men, who were not unaware of this, had decided to take advantage of the situation. Ney and Bernadotte fell back in an attempt to lure the Russians to where the Emperor was waiting for them. By ill luck, one of Bernadotte's couriers was captured by the Russians and revealed the plan, but this did not prevent an

1 Now in East Germany, as are Eisenach, Saalfeld, and Magdeburg
2 Friedrich Ludwig Hohenlohe (1746–1818), Prussian General, defeated at Jena
3 A village 20 kilometres north of Jena
4 All these places are in Poland
5 Levin Leontievitch Bennigsen (1745–1826) had been in the service of Catherine II; he distinguished himself at Eylau and Leipzig.

THE GERMAN ARMY AND OTHERS

1 Prussian fusilier (1806)
2 Prussian musketeer (1806)
3 Prussian grenadier (1806)
4 Danish infantry (1814)
5 Russian grenadier (1806)
6 Hussar, Regiment of Blucher (1806)
7 Prussian bodyguard (1815)
8 Prussian cossack (1813)
9 Prussian grenadier (1815)
10 Prussian rifleman (1815)
11, 12 Prussian Guards (1815)
13 Prussian Guards (1812)

1   2   3   4   5

6   7   8

9   10   11   12   13   41

encounter with the French army at Eylau[1] on 8 February 1807.

Blinded by the wind and the snow, the corps under Augerau was cut to pieces, but Murat arrived at the head of 80 squadrons and broke the enemy's front. Davout's attack on the left flank and Ney's on the right finally made the Russians give way. The battle had been bitter and the carnage terrifying – 50,000 casualties of whom 30,000 were Russians. The horrible scene of the battlefield affected the Emperor deeply. Furthermore "this useless butchery" did not produce the expected results. The Russians were already consolidating at Heilsberg.

Napoleon took advantage of this lull in hostilities to reorganise his army and to train the troops from the Rhine Confederation, from Spain and from France.

In spring, hostilities opened with the taking of Dantzig[2] on 26 May, and after a series of minor engagements culminated in the battle of Friedland[3] on 14 June, the anniversary of Marengo.

The battle started at three o'clock in the morning and ended at half-past ten at night with the decisive defeat of the Russians, who after losing 20,000 men, fled towards the Niemen. Two days later Konigsberg[4] fell, and on 19 June Napoleon marched into Tilsit[5] where, on 7 July, he signed a peace treaty with Alexander I.

Although there had been some doubts after Eylau, the French army's reputation for invincibility was now fully restored

At the insistence of the Czar, the Treaty of Tilsit restored to Prussia part of the territories seized by the Emperor. Prussia, "the martyr of the German fatherland", was reduced nevertheless from 10 million to 6 million souls, and the populace conceived against the French a hatred and a desire for revenge which time did not diminish.

Napoleon was happy to see his dreams come true, and was already looking forward to the time when he would divide the world between himself and the Russians. The two Emperors loved to hear themselves called by their troops "Emperor of the East" and "Emperor of the West". The soldiers, too were happy to fraternise, even after fighting one another to the death. But the last word must go to Captain Coignet who has left us an account of these brotherly demonstrations:

"We received orders to prepare a banquet for the Russian Guards and to put up very long and spacious tents, all with their entrances in line, and fir trees planted outside. One half of our party set off with the officers to scour the countryside, and the other half put up the tents. Eight days and eight leagues of the surrounding country were allowed to prepare for the event and to collect provisions.

"Everyone set off in good order and the same day the provisions were collected. The next day more than fifty laden vehicles arrived in the camp led by peasants, and every one seemed very happy. They were expecting the bullock carts to be kept in camp, but they were released at once, and the peasants jumped for joy.

"On 30 June 1807, we sat down to table at midday. One could not have wanted better decorated tables, with epergnes of turf and fresh flowers. At the back

1 Bagrationovsk, in the U.S.S.R.
2 Gdansk, in Poland
3 Pravdinsk, in the U.S.S.R.
4 Kaliningrad, in the U.S.S.R.
5 Sovietsk, in the U.S.S.R.

BRITISH INFANTRY
1 Marine (1799)
2 Royal Engineers (1813)
3 Private, Bank Volunteers (1804)
4 Royal Scots Fusiliers (1805)
5 Grenadier (1815)
6 Private, Line Regiment (1815)

1

2

3

4

5

6

43

of each tent there were two stars, the names of the two great men in flowers, and the French and Russian flags.

"We set off altogether to meet the guards who arrived in groups. Each one of us took our opposite number by the arm, but as there were more of us than of them there were often two of us to each of them. They were so tall that they could have used us as crutches. As I was the smallest, I only took on one. I had to look up in the air to see his face; I looked like his small son. They seemed confused to see us in such fine turnout, and our immaculate cooks with their white aprons had to be seen to be believed. Nothing was lacking.

"We sat down to dinner, with a guest on each side, and the meal was served in perfect style. It only goes to show the kind of conviviality which exists amongst the men of this world! We gave them spirits to drink, for this was what we normally took with our meals. Before giving it to them, we had to take a sip and then pass them the pewter goblet which held a quarter of a litre. The contents soon disappeared. They swallowed lumps of meat the size of an egg whole. Soon they became distended, so we made signs to them that they could unbutton their coats and we did the same. This made them feel better for under their coats they wore layers of cloth to give them larger chests than in fact they had. It was quite disgusting to see these bits of rag peeling off.

"Two aides-de-camp arrived, one from our Emperor and one from the Emperor of Russia, to warn us not to go away as the two Emperors were about to pay us a visit. When they arrived, our Emperor made a sign with his hand that no one should get up. The two walked around the table, and the Emperor of Russia said to us: 'Grenadiers, you have shown yourselves worthy of your name.'

"After the Emperors had gone, our Russians, at ease once more, set about eating again. We watched them forcing food and drink down their throats, and when they could not swallow one more morsel, what do you think they did? They stuck their fingers down their throats, brought up their dinner, and started eating again. It was quite disgusting to witness such orgies. They did this three times during the banquet. In the evening, we took home those who could stand; the rest we left under the tables. One of our humorists decided to dress up as a Russian, and persuaded one of them to take off his uniform. They exchanged clothes and set off arm in arm. When they got to the main street in Tilsit, our man parted company with the Russian and ran straight into a Russian sergeant whom he failed to salute, so the sergeant gave him a couple of whacks across the shoulders with his stick. Reckoning that he had been assaulted, our man forgot he was disguised, and jumped on the sergeant, knocking him down. He would have killed him if he had not been stopped, even right under the balcony where the two Emperors were watching the jolly scene, which made them laugh heartily. The sergeant was knocked out and everyone was happy, above all the Russian soldiers."

The grand dessein which had been discussed by the Czar and the Emperor involved intensifying the continental blockade against the British and subduing Portugal and Spain.

The French losses, though concealed in the official bulletins, none the less made themselves felt. Napoleon ordered the early call-up of the 1807 and 1808 classes, totalling some 160,000 men.

The bad feeling of these new recruits soon vanished when they met the old soldiers and heard their tales of glory.

BRITISH CAVALRY
1 Dragoon (1815)
2 Royal Horse Guards (1813)
3 Hussar (1815)
4 Light Dragoon (1800)
5 Dragoon (1811)
6 1st Royal Dragoons (1804)

With the *grand dessein* in view, the army under Murat invaded the Peninsula at the beginning of the year 1808. The rising in Madrid on 2 May 1808 took the world by surprise. The Spanish had at last shown themselves a force to be reckoned with. The pitiless suppression that followed, witnessed by Goya, inspired him to make a number of canvases and drawings which show almost morbidly the horrors of war. No sooner was it put down in Madrid, than the revolt spread to the rest of Spain, giving the British the opportunity of intervening in Europe and showing the arrogant French Emperor that Britain had not given up the struggle. One of the generals in the British expedition was Arthur Wellesley, the future Duke of Wellington. No sooner had he left his ship than he defeated Marshal Junot, who surrendered at Sintra on 30 August, seven days after the surrender of 18,000 men under Dupont[1] at Balen. This was only the beginning.

Realising the serious position of his collaborators, Napoleon hurried to the rescue with 175,000 seasoned troops at the beginning of November. He defeated the Spanish army and drove the British army back to their ships on 16 January 1809.

The heroic stand of the Spanish dealt a serious blow to the prestige of the French army. A fifth coalition was made between Britain and Austria.

In the spring of 1809, Austria opened the campaign with 500,000 well-prepared men, while the Spanish army contained the Emperor's best troops. Napoleon called up the 1810 class conscripts, those of the earlier classes, and the German contingents, in all some 300,000 men, but they did not compare with the men of Austerlitz. Nevertheless the enthusiasm of their leader proved infectious, and they emerged

victorious on 6 July 1809, at the end of a brilliantly conducted campaign.

At Wagram,[2] "the battle of the guns", where 96,000 rounds were fired by the French, the opposing forces each numbered 350,000 men, and each side lost 25,000 dead. Napoleon had reached the height of his power and ruled over 70 million people.

It was from this hotch-potch of peoples that in the spring of 1812 he drew the 600,000 men intended to squash Alexander I for daring to order him to evacuate Russia. Avoiding the encounter that Napoleon wanted, Koutousov fell back with his 250,000 men, burning everything behind him. In August the imperial army had already lost 150,000 men from sickness and desertion, as well as at least half its horses.

On 7 September they finally came up against Koutousov who, with 140,000 men, had decided to defend the sacred city of Moscow.

The battle of Borodino[3], where 100,000 were killed, was the most bloody and desperate battle of the war, but, for all that it was not decisive. Moscow was occupied, but was burned on orders from Rostopchine. Amid the ashes lay 20,000 wounded and sick who had been caught in the flames.

Then came the long retreat and the arrival of "General Winter" which helped Koutousov and

1 Pierre Dupont de l'Etang (1765–1840), a general under the Revolution, distinguished himself at Marengo and at Ulm, was dismissed after the surrender of Bailen, and then reinstated by Louis XVIII
2 A town in lower Austria, N.E. of Vienna
3 A village near Moscow. The Battle of Borodino is also called the Battle of the Moscova

FOREIGN ARMIES
1 Swedish cuirassier (1809)
2 Spanish grenadier (1808)
3 Hussar, Regiment of Croÿ (1814)
4 Belgian Legion (1814)
5, 6 Belgian line infantry in the service of Holland (1815)
7 Austrian Landwehr (1809)
8 Spanish sapper (1808)
9 Belgian light cavalryman (1815)
10 Belgian rifleman (1815)
11 Dutch carabinier (1814)

47

his Cossacks snarling at the heels of the 90,000 starving survivors of the splendid Grand Army of the previous spring. Only 45,000 finally got back to Germany.

Once the Emperor got back to France he set about building up a new army, and, strange to relate, he managed to do so; 673,000 men and boys–for this army included in its ranks the "Marie-Louise" conscripts of the 1813 class who were under 20 years of age–who tottered under the weight of their equipment.

Napoleon left Erfurt on 26 April, defeated Blucher at the battle of Lutzen[1] on 2 May, and then emerged victorious in the battle of Bautzen[2] on 21 May. The Russians and the Prussians asked for an armistice. This was signed on 4 June but lasted only until 10 August, when the struggle was renewed, this time with the Swedes and the Austrians on the side of the Russians; 550,000 men were absolutely determined to have done with the tyrant of Europe and his 450,000 soldiers. In the ranks of the latter there were Germans and Italians who were beginning to show the first signs of discouragement.

Forced back at Dresden, the Allies were to have better fortune against the Emperor's lieutenants, and they defeated Macdonald, Oudinot and Ney.

At Leipzig, on 19 October in the space of four days, Napoleon and his 175,000 men held their ground against 350,000 men belonging to the coalition. The French victory was almost certain when the Saxons concentrated their artillery against their old allies and thus decided the outcome of the battle. The French were victorious at Hanau[3], but disaster followed. Perhaps Napoleon lost all by trying to regain everything at once.

In 1815 Napoleon undertook a campaign in France in which 80,000 Frenchmen opposed 250,000 allies. His victories in this campaign included: Saint-Dizier on 27 January, Brienne on 29 January, Champaubert on 10 February, Montmirail on the 11th, Chateau-Thierry on the 12th, Vauchamps on the 14th, Mormant on the 16th, and Montereau on the 18th.

These were followed by Craonne on 7 March and the capture of Rheims on 14 March but he was defeated at Arcis-sur-Aube on 20–21 March, outnumbered three to one.

On 11 July, Napoleon abdicated, abandoned by nearly all his one-time followers. Even the famous Mameluke Roustan deserted his master.

After Napoleon's escape from Elba came the Hundred Days, the last effort of the Emperor, which ended in the final "flight of the eagle" to Waterloo. There on 18 June 1815, Wellington gave the final blow in the fight that had lasted 25 years.

1 In the Halle district, East Germany
2 In the Dresden district, East Germany
3 In West Germany, on the Main near Frankfurt

THE RUSSIAN ARMY
1 Tcherkess horseman
2 Bachkir horseman
3 Cossack (1813)
4 Lancer
5 Infantry of the Line
6 Grenadier
7 Dragoon
8 Cuirassier
9 Hussar

1

2

3

4

5

6

7

8

9

F.F.

49

5 The mid-nineteenth century

At its reorganisation in 1808, the Prussian Army had adopted the shako[1] for the infantry, and the crested helmet[2] for the cavalry, which were copied later by all the German states.

In a spirit of opposition to the French tyranny, symbolised by the gaudy uniforms of the Grand Army, the Prussians chose uniforms of sombre colours: black, dark blue or green, and single-breasted.

The peace of 1815 gave the nations once more the opportunity to restore to their uniforms, at any rate on parade, the rich colours of the past.

Restoration France, by the same token, tried to erase the memory of the exiled emperor with new uniforms. The Swiss regiments appeared once more in red coats with white frogging, shakos with peaks and large badges like the Russians. The grenadiers only resumed their bearskins in 1822, when a sky-blue greatcoat was also introduced. The *Garde Royale* loaded themselves with gold braid and pompoms, as if trying to compete in splendour with the past. The Cuirassiers of the Guard replaced their plumed helmets with crested ones like those formerly worn by the Carabiniers. The light cavalry abandoned their famous colback[3] for a crested helmet like that worn by the Prussians, and donned garance[4] trousers, as did the lancers, together with their green kurtkas[5] with crimson collars.

In 1820 the infantry once again put on blue coats; the epaulettes distinguished the regiments of rifles, carabiniers and light infantry. The garance trousers, coloured with a dye from the Rhone valley, were adopted throughout the French army, and they were discontinued only during the First World War.

However, it was these somewhat ridiculous-looking soldiers who crossed the Bidassoa on 7 April 1823 in an effort to save the throne of King Ferdinand VII of Spain. What a change from the last war with Spain! The Spanish population no longer cut the throats of the injured, but frantically acclaimed the defenders of the legitimate king against the rebels.

1 Head-dress of Hungarian origin, either conical or cylindrical, and with peak.
2 The comb of the helmet is ornamented with a brush-like crest of hair or silk.
3 Fur cap with a plume, brought back from Egypt by Bonaparte's soldiers
4 Red dye obtained from the root of a plant of the same name
5 Polish jacket

THE ROYAL ARMY IN FRANCE (I)
1 Garde du Corps du Roi (1820–1830)
2 Dragoon, Garde Royale (1815–1820)
3 Mounted rifles (1830)
4 Lancer, Garde royale (1816)
5 Garde du Corps du Roi (1820–1830)
6 Mousquetaire gris (1814–1815)

1
2
3
4
5
6

51

Taken over by an audacious blow, the fort of the Trocadero fell on 31 August, and Cadiz followed a few days later. Ferdinand's throne had been saved, and Paris prepared a triumph for its heroes.

Another military intervention, this time against the Turks in 1828, produced still more honours for an army thirsty for glory to rival that of the past.

The memory of the prestigious uniforms of the Grand Army still lived in the minds of the Emperor's most implacable enemies, not the least of which was England.

The first regiments of Lancers in the British Army were introduced in 1816, and they adopted a uniform more or less identical with that of Napoleon's famous Polish Lancers, including the chapska[1] with brass mountings and a flowing plume, while the Hussars had worn trousers and carried curved sabres, inspired by the Imperial Guard's mamelukes, since 1815.

The barracks had changed very little, and life within their walls stayed as unpleasant as it had been in the previous century. A soldier got only two inferior meals a day, morning and midday, which were supplemented by the local shopkeepers, greedy for gain, at exorbitant prices. The cat-o'-nine-tails was used to punish serious breaches of discipline.

Despite these unpleasant conditions, the British soldier remained one of the best in the world. It is true to say that there were plenty of opportunities to gain glory, whether in New Zealand (1845) or in the Cape against the Zulus. These may have been minor wars, but they served to draw attention to the obsolete methods of training and the unsuitability of the uniform.

Equally important were the military operations in India where the "redcoats" covered themselves with glory and gained the admiration of the world in their conflict with an enemy whose courage was equalled by his ferocity.

In the meantime France was preparing for her expedition to Algeria. In 1830; 37,000 men, supported by 103 men o' war, landed at Sidi-Ferruch where, on 19 June, they came up against the Bey's[2] Turkish troops. The stifling heat put this army, dressed for a ceremonial parade in Paris, to the test, but they rose to the occasion when it came to devising a practical head-dress as a protection against the sun. General Bugeaud[3] himself, in defiance of regulations, made himself a cap with large front and back peaks that supplied the subject for a popular song.

1 Square-topped cap: Polish national head-dress
2 Local ruler
3 Thomas-Robert Bugeaud de la Piconnerie, Duc d'Isly (1784–1849), Marshal of France, Governor of Algeria (1840)

THE ROYAL ARMY OF FRANCE (II)

1 Cente-Suisse (1814–1817)
2 Garde de la Porte (1814–1816)
3 Grenadier, Garde royale (1815–1830)
4 Swiss Regiment, Garde royale (1816–1822)
5 Light infantry 76th Departmental Legion (1815–1820)
6 Infantry (1820)
7 Engineers (1845)
8 Infantry (1828)

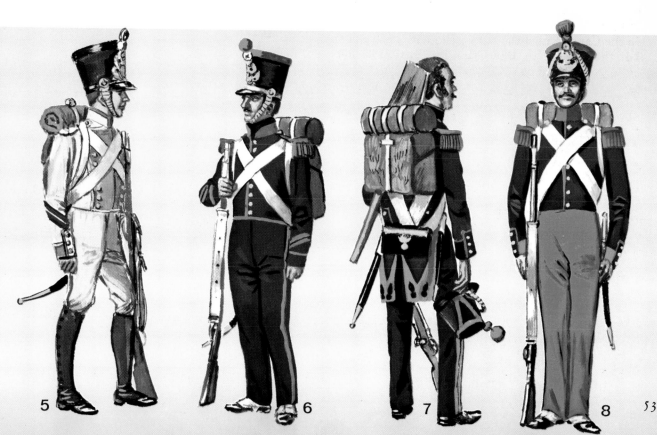

1   2   3   4

5   6   7   8   53

New regiments gradually came into being, among them the startling Zouaves, who were Frenchmen dressed like the bearded Zwawas of Kabylia.

Whether they liked it or not, the army had come under the spell of romanticism which was reflected in the dress. Soon Turcos[1] appeared, then Spahis, who were natives, as distinct from the Chasseurs d'Afrique who were white, and then the Foreign Legion.

The forage cap with a peak added, developed into the kepi, and bolt-operated weapons replaced the old flintlock musket.

An unexpected outcome of the Napoleonic Wars in Spain was that the Spanish colonies in South America tried to throw off the Spanish yoke. During the war in Spain, these colonies had set up their own governments that exercised power in the name of the King of Spain. They found independence very much to their liking, after they had realised the extent to which the decadent Spain of Ferdinand VII had enriched herself at their expense.

The leader of this revolution, Simon Bolivar, a Venezuelan of education and enthusiasm, led the rebels in the north, while San Martin controlled the insurrection in the south.

This revolution, like so many others, had its teething troubles when Spain reacted so quickly. Bolivar's second-in-command, General Miranda, surrendered.

Refusing to become discouraged, Bolivar succeeded in reconquering his country with the help of a small band of brave revolutionaries after an arduous march through the jungle. But *El Libertador* had more troubles ahead, for the evacuation of Spain by the French in 1814 had allowed Ferdinand VII to crush the rebellion at home.

Although checked, Bolivar returned to the fight in 1816; and as his own country was now liberated he decided to attack the Spanish forces in New Grenada[2] in 1819. After a testing march through forest, the foothills of the Andes came in sight, then the peaks, growing higher and higher and colder and colder. At last, reduced to only half their number, Bolivar's little army, now exhausted and starving but still under control, fell upon the dumbfounded royalists, routed them, and marched into Santa Fé de Bogota.

Subjected to strict discipline and with European equipment, using "War to the death" as their war-cry, the revolutionary army liberated Guiana and then Ecuador. In Peru, Bolivar continued the struggle started by San Martin, and on 9 December 1824, his lieutenant Sucre fought a great battle in the plain of Ayacucho, and the royalist army was finally defeated.

1 *Tirailleurs algériens*
2 Colombia

VARIOUS ARMIES

1 Partisan, Carlist, Wars in Spain (1835)
2 Garde du Corps, Baden (1824)
3 Polish Free Corps (1831)
4 Austrian infantry (1830)
5 Spanish light infantry (1830)
6 Mexican infantry (1826)
7 Brasilian infantry (1823)
8 Polish franc-tireur
9 Infantry, Modena (1820)

Although a successful soldier, Bolivar failed in his attempt to bring about federation between the Latin American Republics. He died, a disappointed man, in the new state which he had founded: Columbia.

In Mexico, a priest, Miguel Hidalgo, had also attempted to drive out the Spanish, and left his head planted on a wall for the edification of the rebellious. This unfortunate revolutionary made the mistake of relying on numbers alone—90,000—to overcome 5,000 royalist soldiers, and the affair ended in disaster. Profiting from this lesson, Hidalgo's second in command, Morelos, started by stealing arms from the garrison at Acapulco, and once his army was equipped, he instilled European discipline into it.

A military genius, this half-caste Indian and Negro led three successive campaigns and took all southern Mexico except Mexico City itself, where he was taken prisoner and shot.

Mexico had to wait until 1867 for full liberty, still cut off from Texas, "the republic of the lone star", after the battles of the Alamo and San Jacinto.

In Europe, Poland had risen up against her Russian masters in 1830, but it had been barbarously suppressed over a period of ten months. More fortunate Belgium overcame the Dutch troops and gained her independence. In February 1848 there was yet another revolution, this time in France and King Louis-Philippe fled to England.

Like a tidal wave, liberal ideas swept across Germany, Austria, and Italy where Garibaldi's volunteers were preparing for action. In five days Milan drove out the Austrians under Radetzky, a veteran of Marengo and Wagram. He had his revenge a few months later on 25 July 1848, when he defeated the insurgents at Custozza. No sooner had the Austrians regained control in Italy than the Hungarians in their turn revolted, and liberated their country.

But the Emperor of Russia, Nicholas I, put and end to the valiant Hungarians' hopes of emancipation by sending 80,000 men against them under Paskievitch, the executioner of Warsaw. The Hungarian rising was crushed at Temesvar[1] on 10 August 1849.

Little or no advance was made in the science of warfare until the Crimean War which upset the old ideas of strategy and resulted in far-reaching military reforms.

In France, Louis-Napoleon was elected President, and on 2 December 1852 he became Emperor Napoleon III.

1 Timisoara, in Romania

ENGLISH INFANTRY

1 Light Infantry (1834)
2 Light Infantry (1845)
3 Officer, 13th Light Infantry (1848)
4 The King's Liverpool Regiment (1864)
5 Rifle Volunteers (1860)

1

3

2

4

5

57

This *Bonaparte de petit format* (as Victor Hugo called him) declared "The Empire stands for peace", and then dragged France through a long succession of wars which ended only with his abdication.

The army, which had placed the emperor on the throne, had lost much of its national character and was accused of being nothing more than an expensive toy for the amusement of Napoleon III.

What was more, young men with money could easily avoid military service by finding replacements among young men with no money through special agencies, a proceeding that weakened the sense of duty in French youth.

The art of killing made fair progress, however, thanks to the tremendous growth of the arms industry.

The antiquated flintlock of the musket, which had been in use for two centuries, was superseded by the percussion system of firing, and rifling was introduced, resulting in a breech-loading rifle firing elongated bullets (1836). The artillery had also adopted rifled pieces, which fired time- and percussion-fuse shells, case shot, etc.

Anxious to make his mark, Napoleon III used a dispute between the Catholic and the Orthodox Christians in Palestine as a pretext to bring pressure on the Sultan of Constantinople. The Emperor of Russia, Nicholas I, at once supported the Sultan, delighted at the opportunity of hindering the heir of the man who had tried to conquer Russia.

The truth was that Russia saw in this affair the long-dreamed-of opportunity of acquiring a Mediterranean outlet by liquidating the decadent Ottoman Empire. Napoleon III was too aware of the mistakes made by his uncle, Napoleon I, to risk alienating the English by attacking Turkey. Nicholas I provided the answer for him by invading Moldavia and Walachia in July 1853 and destroying the Turkish fleet in the harbour of Sinope. At the beginning of April 1854 France and Britain joined forces to save the Sultan.

The Allies landed in May 1854 at Gallipoli—30,000 French and 20,000 British—and established a base there. Their leaders soon realised that they had insufficient resources. Then cholera broke out, killing thousands. Meanwhile the Russians withdrew northwards.

On 14 September 1854 a landing was made at Eupatoria with 30,000 French, 20,000 English and 7,000 Turks. They attacked the Russian lines along the Alma on a front of six kilometres. The method of attack was no different from that used in the Napoleonic wars. The British, French and Turks advanced, colours flying and bands playing, led by the light infantry.

BRITISH CAVALRY

1 13th Light Dragoon (1837)
2 Light Dragoon (1850)
3 Hussar (1868)
4 11th Hussars (1850)
5 Hussar (1841)
6 6th Dragoon Guards (1838)

The crossing of the Alma threw this fine display into confusion, and the Allies reached the opposite bank in disorder.

The Russians, manoeuvring in close column and armed with only poor-quality muskets, notwithstanding their undoubted bravery, were forced to take shelter in Sebastopol, having lost 9,000 men. The Allies, who had lost half their men, blamed each other for the mistakes which had been made and took credit for the successes.

The siege of Sebastopol lasted nearly a year, and the Russians put up a most stubborn defence. But the terrible winter of 1854–1855 proved even worse for the Allies, now decimated by dysentery and cholera. It was then that the name of a woman, Florence Nightingale, became better known that that of any of the military leaders.

This celebrated nurse had been sent to Scutari where a military hospital for treating the wounded had been set up. Everything was lacking–doctors, medicine, dressings, anaesthetics. Furthermore, dirt and vermin had invaded the area to such an extent that more men died of infection than of wounds. Florence Nightingale lashed out against those responsible, the indifferent and unintelligent officials who sheltered behind regulations. Backed up by the army surgeons, this determined lady obtained clean sheets, decent meals, and even knives and forks. Filth gave place to cleanliness, and the hell that was Scutari became a haven of mercy.

"God bless Miss Nightingale," sang the people back in England. "May she be free from strife."

Less spectacular, but still important in the history of warfare, was the appearance of the first war correspondents, who sent their news by telegraph. Photographs, taken by an Englishman, Roger Fenton, have preserved for us an authentic record of the Crimean War.

The siege continued, despite sustained attacks of the Russian relief force under Mantschikov. One sortie against the English base by these troops resulted in the famous "Charge of the Light Brigade", which has gone down in history as an example of discipline.

The British cavalry, led by Lord Cardigan, charged down a valley dominated by the Russian artillery and infantry. The Light Brigade consisted of the 4th, 8th and 11th Hussars, the 13th Light Dragoons and the 17th Lancers. At first nonplussed by this suicidal charge, the Russians eventually opened rapid fire on the cavalry, who were decimated and only saved from total massacre by a diversion by the French 4th Chasseurs d'Afrique.

Contrary to expectations, the British losses proved not as heavy as had been feared: out of 673 men, 113 had been killed and 134 wounded. The figures were later exaggerated raising the number

VARIOUS ARMIES
1 Belgian grenadier (1830)
2 Hungarian infantry (1850)
3 Infantry, Republic of Lombardy (1848)
4 Danish artillery (1848)
5 Polish grenadier (1831)
6 Neapolitan lancer (1840)
7 Belgian mounted rifles (1831)
8 Spanish cuirassier (1845)

of dead to 505. Whatever else might be the case, the British army had shown the enemy that it was not to be intimidated. The allies gained the advantage in the end by a victorious charge of the Heavy Brigade made up of the Royals, the Greys, the Inniskillings and the 4th and 5th Dragoon Guards. This 800-strong cavalry force broke up 3,000 Russian cavalry, putting them to flight and inflicting heavy losses.

During this time, the siege was carried with the usual approach works and heavy bombardments. An innovation was the use of snipers, camouflaged and armed with rifles with telescopic sights. The furtive nature of this new method of warfare, which smacked of premeditated murder, earned the snipers the contempt of the rest of the troops, just as the first arquebusiers had.

At Inkerman, on 5 November 1854, just before dawn and in thick fog, the Russians attacked the British positions held by Lord Raglan.

Taken by surprise, the British wavered at first but then rallied. They stemmed the attack and eventually counter-attacked the Russians on the flanks. The thick fog enabled the British to conceal their weakness in numbers. The French, under Canrobert, arrived to reinforce the Allies, and the combined efforts of the two armies finally overcame the Russian resistance. The Russians fell back in disorder in the face of bayonet charges and took shelter in Sebastopol, leaving 12,000 of their men on the battlefield.

The siege of Sebastopol was intensified, and the famous Russian bastion at Malakov became the main objective. The French, whose new commander-in-chief, Marshal Pélissier, had hitherto disregarded the plans evolved by Napoleon III, failed in an initial assault on their fort. Finally, after a terrible bombardment, the French planted the tricolour on the Malakov, so gaining control over the whole harbour with their guns. The Russians were at last beaten, and the French soldier looked upon himself as the best soldier in the world. It was an honour gained at a cost of 100,000 killed and wounded.

The Allies parted on terms of mutual recrimination, blaming one another for the mistakes made during this bloody campaign.

An unusual event was that the victors marched past the enemy commander-in-chief. They took home with them a thing that was soon to enjoy immense popularity, the cigarette.

No sooner was the Treaty of Paris signed in March 1856, than another war broke out, this time in Italy.

Camillo de Cavour, who had sent a contingent from Piedmont to fight with the Allies in the Crimean War, had dreams of liberating Italy. His wishes were fulfilled when, in April 1859, Austria issued an ultimatum. Thirsting for war, Napoleon II immediately sprang

GERMAN ARMY

1, 2 Prussian (1830)
3 German artillery (1835)
4 Mecklenburg musketeer (1830)
5 Prussian Uhlan (1821)
6 Prussian Hussar (1832)
7 Prussian rifleman (1845)
8 Prussian grenadier (1845)

1

5

2

3

4

6

7

8

to the help of his tiny ally Sardinia, which had been invaded by the army of Franz-Joseph.

In France, mobilisation took place amid disorder. Somehow the army reached Italy, and only on the eve of the battle of Solferino had it been brought to full strength.

In this campaign, the French infantry had covered themselves with glory. Laden like mules [their packs contained their jackets, shoes, pants, shirts, brushes, camp kit, blanket, tent pegs, mess tins, water bottles, entrenching tools, five days' rations and 80 rounds of ammunition], they had defeated the Austrians at Montobello, Palestro, Turbigo, and Magenta.

These victories were gained without any preparation, and carried by famous bayonet charges, very much like those of the soldiers of the Revolution. This deluded the French army into believing in its own invincibility and relying simply on the bayonet.

Drunk with glory, and just as incompetent as his adversary Franz-Joseph, Napoleon III continued his triumphant march to the accompaniment of frenzied acclamation by the liberated Italians. On 24 June 1859 the two sides met at Solferino: 135,000 allies against 135,000 Austrians, who in fact comprised a variety of nationalities. They were good soldiers, and were armed with Lorenz rifles.

Here again there was no preparation before the battle. The two sides fell upon each other, firing shots here and there, until Franz-Joseph ordered the retreat.

Napoleon III, though an execrable tactician, on this occasion displayed the greatest courage and disregard for personal safety.

In the midst of the conflict, a civilian hurried about the battlefield tending the wounded as best he could, and setting up an improvised medical service. His name was Jean Henri Dunant, and he was a young Swiss banker. The lessons of the Crimean campaign had not yet borne fruit, and the majority of the 40,000 wounded lay helpless, calling in vain for assistance. Dunant wrote a book about what he had seen and urged the nations to set up relief societies which would help the wounded in war-time. A body of Swiss citizens met in Geneva to discuss the proposal, and this was followed by an international conference in 1864 and the Convention of Geneva, which saw the founding of Red Cross Societies. An emblem was wanted, and in honour of Switzerland this was a red cross on a white ground, obtained by reversing the colours on the Swiss flag. (In some eastern countries the emblem is the Red Crescent.)

The Peace of Zurich put an end to the war between France and Austria; and thanks to Garibaldi and his "Red Shirts" the Italians proclaimed Victor-Emmanuel King of Italy in 1861.

VARIOUS ARMIES
1 Romania (1850)
2 Austria (1848)
3 Portugal (1855)
4 U.S.A. (1851)
5 Austrian light cavalry (1850)
6 Argentine (1865)
7 Mexico (1863)
8 Belgium (1857)
9 Belgian cuirassier (1862)
10 Belgian Legion, Mexico (1864)

Meanwhile, Prussia was building up a superbly trained army of young, hand-picked soldiers, utilising the whole national effort. The artillery was strengthened by the new breech-loading, quick-firing, Krupp gun. The Prussian army, 500,000 strong, could find a total of a million well-trained men by calling up its reserves.

In 1861 Mexico, which had suffered a succession of revolutions, then had as president the energetic Benito Juarez. Under the pretext of protecting their own interests, Britain, France and Spain sent out troops to Mexico. After a time, France, with the intention of replacing the Juarez regime by a monarch, hit upon Maximilian of Austria, Franz-Joseph's brother, as the best candidate for the throne.

The Mexican venture got off to a good start: the 30,000 men of the French expeditionary force conquered Mexico and duly installed the emperor.

Maximilian had married Charlottle of Belgium, and a Belgian company was sent out to serve as her Imperial Guard. But soon there were setbacks. At Camaron, the 1st Battalion of the French Foreign Legion fought its last battle. Sixty-six legionnaires held their own against 1,500 dissidents, fighting to the last man. Under pressure from the United States, Napoleon III recalled his troops and abandoned Maximilian, who was captured by Juarez and shot on 19 June 1867.

Meanwhile Prussia, intent on imposing her leadership in Germany, had wiped out the Austrians at Sadowa[1] on 3 July 1866. The Ems Despatch, falsified by Bismark, gave Prussia the opportunity to try her strength against her hereditary enemy.

1 Sadova, in Czechoslovakia

RUSSIAN ARMY

1 Horse Grenadier of the Guard (1850)
2, 3 Cuirassiers of the Guard (1850)
4 Garde du Corps (1830)
5 Garde du Corps (1831)
6 Marine, artillery (1845)
7 Grenadier (1845)

This war, which was to have immense repercussions and which led eventually to the two World Wars, started favourably for the French. France declared war on Prussia on 17 July 1870, and the people of Paris set up the cry of "To Berlin!", certain of a spectacular and rapid victory.

On 2 August a French reconnaissance towards Sarrebruck penetrated into Lorraine. The only consequence was the scattering of one battalion of infantry and three squadrons of cavalry. Count Zeppelin escaped the light cavalry only by having resort to his pistol.

On 4 August in Alsace, there was a much more serious affair when 5,000 French were attacked by 40,000 Prussians and Bavarians of the Third Army. Taken by surprise during dinner, the French fell back on the slopes of Geissberg[1]. They lost 1,200 of their own men, and killed 1,500 of the enemy.

These 270,000 men, raised in great haste instead of the planned 500,000, were doomed to be beaten by an enemy of twice their strength, who had devoted much time to preparation. The inferiority of the Dreyse rifle used by the Germans, compared with the French Chassepôt guns with firing pins, was compensated for by the excellent Krupp gun, which had a range of 2,500 metres and fired deadly percussion shells.

On 6 August the Germans launched simultaneous attacks on Alsace and Lorraine, defeating MacMahon at Froeschwiller and Frossard at Forbach.

On the front, MacMahon's 46,000 men had vainly put into practice their leader's celebrated motto, *J'y suis, j'y reste* ("I stay where I am"), by resisting without hope of reinforcement the successive attacks of 125,000 men under the Crown Prince of Prussia, sacrificing the cuirassiers and the lancers of the Michel brigade to no purpose. On the other front, the 29,000 men of the 2nd Corps were beaten by force of numbers after an heroic resistance against 70,000, and withdrew towards Metz.

Meanwhile, as the result of unbelievable incompetence, the corps under Bazaine, Ladmirault, and Bourbaki withdrew into the stronghold of Metz instead of going to the help of their unfortunate countrymen.

1 South of Wissembourg, Département Bas-Rhin

FRENCH INFANTRY, 1870

1 Infantry of the Line
2 Zouave
3 Grenadier of the Guard
4 Chasseur à pied
5 Marine
6 Garde mobile, Department of the Seine
7 Pontifical Zouave
8 Garibaldi's Red Shirts
9 French Chassepôt rifle

1   2   3   4

9

5   6   7   8   69

But all was not yet lost: a single capable leader could have changed the whole course of the war. Unfortunately the Emperor, now both ill and discouraged, pinned his faith on Bazaine, and entrusted him with the task of uniting the Rhine Army with that of MacMahon, to halt the German advance on Paris. But Bazaine disobeyed his orders. Intending to act on his own and at the right moment, he succeeded only in falling into the trap carefully laid by the enemy around Metz.

Mazaine's army began its retreat to Verdun too late and too slowly, and was caught by von Miltke's advance elements on 14 August. The French broke the German attack, but they had lost yet another day. On 16 August the Germans attacked once more what they took for the French rearguard. Bazaine let slip through his fingers a unique opportunity to inflict a heavy defeat on the German advanced guard, who were numerically weaker than the 125,000 Frenchmen all ready for battle. After several hours of bitter fighting at Rezonville the Germans proceeded to cut off Bazaine's route to Verdun.

On 18 August the French army fought at Saint-Privat[1], without their commander bestirring himself. Again the bravery and dedication of the soldiers availed nothing: for lack of ammunition Canrobert was forced to fall back and abandon Saint-Privat to the Germans.

The army fell back on Metz. From now on the French were cornered, having lost 30,000 of their own men, although they had inflicted heavy losses on the Germans who lost 38,000 killed and wounded, including many of the famous Prussian Guard.

MacMahon also retired there after his 140,000 men had consolidated at Chalons after the defeat at Froeschwiller. The Marshal lost his head and retreated for ten days before he realised that the enemy were not pursuing him.

This was the man to whom the government was to entrust the task of raising the blockade on Metz, whence Bazaine had tried to break out on 12 August. Although this project was meant to be kept secret, it was thoughtlessly told to the press, who equally foolishly commented complaisantly on the situation in the columns of their newspapers.

1 Saint-Privat-la-Montagne in Moselle

FRENCH CAVALRY, 1870

1 Cuirassier
2 Dragoon
3 Mounted rifles
4 Artillery of the Guard
5 Lancer
6 Cuirassier of the Guard
7 Hussar
8 Artillery

1   2   3   4

5   6   7   8

The German staff no doubt laughed heartily, but they were not slow to take advantage of such providential information.

The German troops had no difficulty in outstripping the incredibly slow progress of the relief force, and inflicted serious losses at Beaumont,[1] where on 30 August the French lost 5,000 through the negligence of one of their generals.

MacMahon decided to concentrate his troops at Desan, little thinking that he was condemning them to destruction. On 31 August, 240,000 Germans began to surround the 124,000 French caught in the trap. By the time MacMahon had realised his error it was too late, and a final attempt to escape towards Mezieres failed. Despite an heroic charge by the Chasseurs d'Afrique and the Hussars, which earned the admiration of the King of Prussia himself, disaster was inevitable. The disorganised army fell back on Sedan under German artillery fire.

On 2 September, Napoleon III tried in vain to negotiate with William of Prussia; Bismark and Moltke insisted on unconditional surrender. The entire French army, including the Emperor himself, were to lay down their arms and be sent to various Prussian fortresses. Alsace and most of Lorraine were to be ceded to the victor, and an indemnity of 4,000,000,000 francs was to be paid. The disaster was completed by Bazaine who, at Metz on 27 October, surrendered with 173,000 men and all arms, equipment and stores.

And so, in less than three months, Prussia and her German allies had annihilated the organised forces of France. Contrary to expectation, the French people, in a burst of patriotism, held out for another four months against the invaders.

The Empress Eugenie surreptitiously fled from Paris to England and the republican party deprived Louis-Napoleon Bonaparte and his heirs of the succession for ever.

A "Government for the National Defence" under the direction of Gambetta was created to save the honour of the French nation. Several weeks after the disaster of Sedan, the Germans began the siege of Paris, where two million inhabitants endured the pangs of hunger. The leaders of the new government realised that it was

1 About twenty kilometres south-east of Sedan

GERMAN INFANTRY

1 Rifleman of the Guard
2 Bavarian rifleman
3 Saxon rifleman
4 Württemberg infantry
5 Saxon fusilier
6 Landwehr rifleman
7 Prussian infantry
8 Prussian Grenadier of the Guard
9 German Dreyse rifle

useless to try further to resist the exorbitant demands of the invader, but the ebullient Gambetta was determined to reawaken the revolutionary spirit of 1792, and he escaped from Paris in a balloon in order to organise resistance in the provinces. Meanwhile, the methodical Prussians had surrounded the capital with a system of trenches and redoubts connected with one another by telegraph.

In November and December the Parisians attempted massive sorties which were all repulsed with considerable losses, despite heroic efforts to break the iron ring of 300,000 enemy and 900 guns surrounding them.

The famine soon became acute, the bread ration was cut to 300 grams, and the meat ration to 30 grams. The poor of Paris were dying in hundreds. The relief forces mustered by Gambetta had meantime attacked along the Loire, in Picardy and in Normandy, as well as in Bourgogne and in Franch-Compte. This army consisted of an assortment of troops, the mobile guard, recruits, National Guards, all under the command of an improvised corps of officers, and foreign volunteers such as the Pontifical Zouaves and Garibaldi's "Red Shirts". Numerous bodies of *francs-tireurs* were formed. These armies fought to their utmost but were compelled to submit to the enemy who drove them back on all sides, not without suffering severe losses themselves. The armstice was finally concluded on 28 January 1871.

Ten days later the German Emperor was crowned at the Palace of Versailles. The great masquerade in the Hall of Mirrors (as Bronsart von Schellendorf, a Prussian officer called it) gave birth to the First German Reich.

GERMAN CAVALRY

1 Death's-Head Hussars
2 Dragoon
3 Hussar
4 Bavarian Light Cavalry
5 Württemberg Cavalry
6 Württemberg Heavy Cavalry
7 Prussian cuirassier
8 Uhlan
9 Mecklenburg dragoon
10 Military police

74

7 The American Civil War

While Europe was involved in a long series of wars during the first half of the 19th Century, the American nation carried on with its march towards a great future. Nevertheless, towards the middle of the century, a quarrel developed between the states in the north and those in the south. The north had become highly industrialised through the efforts of the businessmen who were as avid for gain as for success, whereas the south had concentrated on agriculture, principally cotton-growing, which formed the basis of its economy.

An apparently innocuous novel revived the long-standing quarrel in which the question of Negro slavery in the south was not the only bone of contention. Harriet Beecher-Stowe's *Uncle Tom's Cabin* stirred up world-wide indignation and pity in the cause of the slaves, and gave new life to the bitter reproaches made by the northern democrats. They claimed that the aristocratic and indolent south was infringing the Constitution and was bitterly opposing import taxes which were designed to protect American industry but which would have dealt a severe blow to the economy of the agricultural regions.

The southerners saw a solution to the problem which seemed ideal to their eyes: to form a republic made up of Virginia, South Carolina, Georgia, Kentucky, Tennessee, Florida, Alabama, Louisiana and Texas.

The election of the new President of the United States in 1860 put a match to the fuse. Abraham Lincoln was loathed by the southerners, who immediately formed the Confederate States of America under the presidency of Jefferson Davis.

From this moment on, nothing could bring a halt to the bloody war which broke out between the Unionists and the Confederates.

Fort Sumter was besieged by the southerners on 12 April 1861, and surrendered two days later. North Carolina and Arkansas now joined the Confederation, making a total of eleven Southern States opposing the 23 states of the Union. The northerners marched off to make the southerners see sense, convinced that the campaign would last no more than a few months, but they had underestimated the enemy resources, which compensated their inferior numbers by an unexpected energy and determination.

Although better organised than the Confederate army, the northern army, like the southern, lacked experienced leaders. However, it did have the enormous advantage of industrial backing and experience.

The northern army's objective was Richmond, the Confederate capital. The first battle of a war which was to last for four years took place on the banks of the Bull Run River on 21 July 1861.

An event probably unique in the annals of war was that hundreds of civilians from the little town of

AMERICAN CIVIL WAR
–FEDERAL ARMY

1 Artillery officer
2 Cavalry
3 New York Zouave
4 Infantry
5 Soldier, 7th Regiment of New York

Manassas sat down comfortably on the surrounding hills to see the battle. From being spectators they found themselves transformed into actors when the northerners dragged them with them in a helter-skelter retreat after the battle went against them. The southerners were victorious and settled down to rest on their laurels, but the northerners had learnt their lesson and, henceforth, they maintained a well-trained army which had nothing in common with the romantic ideas of the early days of the conflict.

President Lincoln mustered an army of 500,000 men under General MacClellan; it was called the Army of the Potomac. Congress ordered the blockade of the southern states. The southerners, without considering the implications of these sanctions, sent an army to the Potomac where the northerners were massing for an early attack.

In the spring of 1862 MacClellan decided to resume operations against Richmond. No sooner had he taken the enemy capital than he received alarming news from his own side: on the orders of General Jackson, the forces defending Washington had been attacked and destroyed by a southern army.

Jackson joined with General Lee at Richmond to attack MacClellan, who retreated in a hurry. On 30 August, the second battle at Bull Run proved yet another defeat for the north, but at Antietam the southerners were forced to withdraw. It was at this point that a northern General appeared who was to become a national hero: Ulysses S. Grant. He was a professional soldier who did not enjoy a particularly good reputation, and was accused among other things of being an inveterate drinker.

The year 1863 marked the turning point in the Civil War. Since the battle of Fredericksburg in December 1862, the northerners suffered a number of reverses until July 1863 when Lee, victorious but deprived of Jackson's support, met the northern army at Gettysburg.

The most famous battle of the whole war ran in favour of Lee at first, and, after two days of bitter fighting, he could hope for victory, but on 3 July the northern artillery decided the outcome of the bloody battle. On the following day, Lee was forced to retreat from the Union.

On 4 July the stronghold at Vicksburg fell to General Grant, who now held the entire Mississippi valley. He proved himself as a leader by the victory of Chattanooga several months later and was made supreme commander of the army.

Supported by General Sherman, famous for his severity towards the civilian population, Grant took Lee's surrender at Appomattox on 9 April 1865.

Victory finally came to the side better equipped as well as being the richer. So ended the first industrial war!

AMERICAN CIVIL WAR –CONFEDERATE ARMY

1 Special corps in the Black cavalry
2 Cavalry officer
3 Artillery
4, 5, 6 Types of infantry
7 Bombardier, artillery
8 Naval Colt pistol, 1851
9 Naval Colt pistol 1851, with carbine butt
10 Sharp's carbine
11 Infantry rifle

8 The Imperial armies

After the Crimean War, Russia joined the other countries of Europe in the general colonial expansion, seeking to find in Asia some consolation for her defeat.

In 1839 war broke out between China and Great Britain. The British quickly got the upper hand, to the extent of threatening Nanking. With no modern arms, the Chinese soldiers were unable to stand up to the British forces, and the Emperor was finally compelled to allow the British to use the naval bases and to cede Hong Kong.

Two years later the United States, France, Russia and several other countries also extracted concessions from the weak Manchu Emperor.

Japan also excited the cupidity of the Western world but was able to withstand the pressure, and yielded nothing beyond a few trade concessions.

In India the British had to contend with frequent uprisings. In Afghanistan, the campaign of 1839–42 proved disastrous but showed up the weak points in the tactics employed in a warfare where ambush played an important part.

In 1845 the Sikhs, a war-like race from the Punjab, mustered 60,000 men with western arms and equipment and trained by French and Italian officers. Their objective was Delhi. The first days of battle, which lasted until nightfall, showed the Sikhs to be a match for the British troops. But a British attack in the early hours of the following morning was successful, and the Sikhs retreated, leaving behind their artillery and baggage. A second army soon came to their rescue and made repeated attacks on the 18,000 British troops, but finally gave way and fled in disorder under the threat of a British cavalry charge. The Sikhs were

FRENCH INFANTRY AT THE END OF THE 19TH CENTURY

1 Gunner
2 Marine Infantry
3 Tirailleur algérien
4 Chasseur alpin
5 Engineer
6 Chausseur à pied
7 Foreign Legion
8 Zouave
9 Infantry of the Line

gallant and well-disciplined, but they lacked capable leaders. Their troops, who were as brave as the British and three times as numerous, were unable to defeat the British, although the latter were exhausted after forty hours' battle in the burning heat, with nothing either to eat or drink.

The war carried on into 1846, and the Sikhs continued fighting with great bravery. They disregarded traditional tactics. For example, infantry charged with the bayonet ahead of the cavalry, and they drew up their battalions in triangular formation so that only the apex of the triangle was exposed to the enemy charge. On other occasions they lay flat on the ground and let the cavalry charge over them, then stood up and fired into the back of the enemy charge.

Defeated at Sobraon, Ramnagar, Chillianwallah and Goojerat in 1849, the Sikhs were later to fight alongside the British troops in the mutiny of the Bengal army (the Indian Mutiny). The Crown gained not only these first-class soldiers but also the famous Koh-i-Noor diamond.[1]

The mutiny in Bengal resulted from the British defeats in Afghanistan and the unsatisfactory outcome of the Crimean War. Agitators thought they saw signs of decline in the British army, an impression strengthened by the relative mildness of the colonial regime compared with the tyranny of the former native rulers.

The matter of the cartridges supplied the agitators with a suitable excuse. The ammunition used with the new Enfield rifle was made up in paper coated with either pork or beef fat, which had to be torn with the teeth so that the powder and the bullet could be taken out.

1 A diamond, the name meaning "mountain of light". It was presented to Queen Victoria, and still forms part of the British Crown Jewels.

FRENCH CAVALRY AT THE END OF THE 19TH CENTURY

1 Officer of Cuirassiers
2 Officer of Hussars
3 Officer of Light Cavalry
4 Chasseur d'Afrique
5 Officer of Dragoons
6 Cuirassier
7 Light cavalryman
8 Dragoon

Word was immediately put around that this was simply a means devised by the British of insulting the native religions and of converting the Indians to Christianity. The pig was considered unclean by the Moslems and the cow was held sacred by the Hindus.

Chappaties (wheat cakes) were distributed to the people; it had been arranged earlier that this was to be the signal for the uprising. On 10 May 1857 the British in Meerut, men, women and children, were massacred by the mutineers. The same thing happened in Cawnpore soon afterwards, and this kindled in the hearts of the British soldiers a desire for vengeance.

Reinforcements from Europe arrived after a four months' journey, for the Suez Canal had not yet been opened.

With skilled commanders, the British at once formulated a plan of campaign. Their long columns marched off to the cry of "Remember Cawnpore", to repay massacre with massacre.

The mutineers' headquarters were at Delhi, the city of the last of the Grand Moguls, and Jhansi was also a dangerous hideout. The latter was the first city to be attacked; 1,500 soldiers, of whom only 500 were British, confronted 22,000 fanatics in their stronghold, dislodged them, and put them to flight.

The siege of Delhi lasted longer. The besiegers defeated all attempts by the mutineers to break out, but they were unable to mount a successful assault with their small force of 4,000 men, more than half of whom were sick, until another column came to their rescue. These reinforcements broke through a force sent to intercept them and brought up siege artillery. After three days' bombardment, the British launched their attack on the shattered bastions, fighting hand to hand.

BRITISH ARMY AT THE END OF THE 19TH CENTURY
1 Officer, Royal Engineers (1895)
2 2nd Queen's Regiment (1895)
3 Fusilier
4 Skinner's Horse
5 Officer, 10th Hussars
6 British Infantry, tropical dress
7 Officer during Boer War
8 Officer, London Scottish Regiment (1890)
9 Officer, Highland Light Infantry (1897)

85

The capture of Delhi marked the first step towards victory, but the war lasted until July 1859. Then repression began.

In China, the Tae-pings had also attempted an uprising against the Emperor who had allowed Westerners to establish themselves in the country.

On 8 October 1860, British and French troops looted and burned the Summer Palace in Peking, in retaliation for the massacre of the plenipotentiaries. The Russians received their share, and founded Vladivostok. France acquired what became the Indo-Chinese Union, consisting of Tonkin, Annam, Laos, Cochin China and Cambodia, and the British occupied Burma.

Next, Japan entered the lists, and with her army of 232,000 men trained by the Germans, put down a revolt in Korea. Then the Japanese declared war on China, and invaded the "Celestial Empire". Only strong protests from France, Britain and Russia halted them, and they had to withdraw, retaining only Formosa. Chinese secret societies with xenophobic leanings such as the sect of the "Grand Couteau", still sought to save China by expelling foreigners.

A League of United Patriots, mistranslated into English as "Boxers", sparked off the rebellion. An international expeditionary force of 18,000 men came to the assistance of the besieged legations. The German Emperor, William II, urged his men to live up to their reputation as Huns! One sector of Peking was allocated to each nation represented. What followed made many a European witness blush for shame.

Two years earlier, the United States had declared war on Spain because of the loss of one of their battleships, the *Maine*, which had sunk in mysterious circumstances in the harbour at Havana.

THE GERMAN ARMY AT THE END OF THE 19TH CENTURY
1 Hussar
2 Kettledrummer, Garde du Corps, Prussia
3 Uhlan (1890)
4 Prussian Hussar (1890)
5 Pomeranian artilleryman (1890)
6 Brandenburg rifleman (1890)
7 Prussian Landwehr (1890)
8 Grenadier of the Guard (1890)
9 Infantry of the Line (1890)

After a short campaign, Spain ceded the Philippines to the United States in return for the sum of $20,000,000 and granted independence to Cuba, where Theodore Roosevelt had distinguished himself at the head of his volunteers. Influenced by the European appetite for conquest, the United States also became a colonial power, and annexed the islands of Hawaii and Puerto Rico.

At the same time, an Anglo-Egyptian army under Kitchener undertook the conquest of Sudan, which had risen up under the Mahdi against Egypt and her British ally, and had murdered General Gordon during the siege of Khartoum. The dervishes were defeated at Omdurman on 2 September 1898. The first machine-gun had just appeared on the battlefield, the invention of an American, Hiram Maxim. The introduction of smokeless powder solved the problem of the smoke-screen that had hitherto resulted from rapid fire.

Khaki replaced the brightly coloured uniforms and observation balloons were used for the first time in the British army.

The victory of Omdurman over the dervishes showed the superiority of modern arms over sheer weight of numbers. The British inflicted 25,000 casualties on the enemy for the 450 men killed. A young lieutenant of Hussars took part in this battle. His name was Winston Churchill.

From now on, war lost its glamour as modern methods were introduced and new engines of destruction perfected.

The discovery of gold in the Transvaal lured the fortune-seekers to the tiny Boer republic, until then too poor to be of any interest. Overnight the big influx of foreign adventurers who came to exploit the mineral resources made Johannesburg a city as corrupt as it was densely populated. However, President Kruger

OTHER ARMIES AT THE END OF THE 19TH CENTURY (I)

1 Officer, Italian light cavalry (1890)
2 Trumpeter, Austrian Hussars (1890)
3 Officer, Swiss Infantry (1894)
4 Officer, Spanish Hussars (1897)
5 Italian Bersaglieri (1890)
6 Italian carabinier on foot (1890)
7 Arcieven-Leibgarde, Austria, Hungary
8 American cavalry (1899)
9 American infantry (1899)

refused these immigrants political rights, while taxing them heavily, an act which fanned the flames of discontent.

Cecil Rhodes, Prime Minister of the Cape Colony, dreamed of extending the Empire in the belief that the more colonies Britain had the greater would be the chances of world peace.

Now the puritanical Kruger made clear his intention to achieve full independence for the Transvaal. Rhodes made the first move and entrusted his friend, Dr. Jameson, with the task of going into the Transvaal in support of the immigrant uprising. Jameson's raid failed miserably, and the participants were captured by the Boers on 2 January 1896. In international terms, this trivial incident assumed an enormous importance when the German Emperor declared his support for Kruger who, being under no illusions, had prepared for the worst.

The Republic of the Transvaal ordered rifles and guns from Creusot; and in Germany a corps of European volunteers hastened to place themselves at the disposal of the Boers. On 10 October 1899 President Kruger issued an ultimatum which was at once rejected. War was declared, and again the unnecessary killing began. At first the Boers had a number of successes. They laid siege to Ladysmith, Kimberley, and Mafeking, where Baden-Powell and his scouts distinguished themselves, and for a time they enjoyed the advantages of superior numbers and an intimate knowledge of the country. They were excellent horsemen and skilled marksmen. Their bullets took their toll of the "red coats" who provided ideal targets with their spiked helmets which had been adopted in 1878 as a result of the victory of the Germans over the French in 1871.

Several other countries, particularly in South America, and for the same reason, adopted the German style of military dress, including the *Pickelhaube*.

OTHER ARMIES AT THE END OF THE 19TH CENTURY (II)
1 Spanish light cavalry (1890)
2 Colonel, Spanish lancers (1890)
3 Italian artillery (1890)
4 Spanish infantry (1890)
5 Officer, Russian Guard Artillery (1890)
6 Grenadier, Russian Palace Guard

The Boers' favourite form of warfare was the ambush. They understood the importance of making use of the ground, and they dug trenches which gave them all-round fire as well as cover from enemy shrapnel.

The British quickly realised the unsuitability of the red coat and, following the example of the troops in Sudan, adopted khaki. The kilt, worn by the Highland Regiments, also proved to be impracticable because a soldier lying on his stomach in the sun for hours on end, got the backs of his legs burned.

Carrier pigeons were used for the first time by the British troops besieged in Mafeking, and the telegraph and telephone came into everyday use.

Armoured trains were introduced, together with blockhouses which defended the roads against the Boer commandos. These blockhouses were equipped with powerful searchlights and surrounded with barbed wire.

Soon the British, 450,000 strong, gained the upper hand and crushed the obstinate resistance of the Boers. After systematically burning the crops and farms, and interning civilians in concentration camps where the mortality rate was unnecessarily high, the British army at last was able to compel the remaining groups of Boers to give in.

On 31 May 1902 peace was concluded honourably with the Transvaal and her ally the Orange Free State, which at last made a a reconciliation possible.

In 1904 war broke out again in Asia. This time the protagonists were the giant Russia and the dwarf Japan, and, contrary to expectations, the dwarf defeated the giant. The antiquated Russian Navy was annihilated by the modern Japanese fleet under

ARMIES IN LATE 19TH CENTURY AND EARLY 20TH CENTURY (I)

1 Belgian grenadier (1885)
2 Belgian carabinier (1885)
3 Belgian guide (1896)
4 Norwegian infantry (1903)
5 Danish engineer (1890)

1

2

3

4

5

Admiral Togo. On land, the Russian Imperial Army was defeated at Mukden on 7 March 1905, and the Czar was compelled to cede Port Arthur and to evacute Manchuria.

Meanwhile the Russian people, alarmed at the disasters of the war, rose in revolt. On 22 January 1905 the army fired into the crowd, and this "Bloody Sunday" triggered off a series of strikes and troubles which ended in six days of fighting in the streets of Moscow in December. In May 1906 further outbreaks of trouble were immediately suppressed. After this there was calm until Russia entered the war and suffered the defeats of 1915.

Austria, now almost forgotten but egged on by the German Emperor, was soon destined to spark off a cataclysmic conflict.

On 5 October 1908, the Emperor Francis Joseph annexed Bosnia and Herzegovina which had been granted to him by the Congress of Berlin in 1878. The moment was well chosen, for the Turks were endeavouring to rid themselves of the tyrant Abdoul Hamid. Italy took advantage of the situation to seize Tripoli, Rhodes and the Dodecanese. Bulgaria, Serbia, Greece and Montenegro soon followed suit. The Balkan countries were also interested in these Turkish spoils, and in the summer of 1913 war broke out; first Serbia and Greece, and then Romania, joined forces against Bulgaria.

The assassination on 28 June 1914 of the Austrian heir-apparent, the Archduke Franz Ferdinand, at Sarajevo resulted in an Austrian ultimatum to Serbia. The stage was set and the curtain went up on one of the greatest tragedies the world has ever known.

ARMIES IN LATE 19TH CENTURY AND EARLY 20TH CENTURY (II)

1 Turkey (1890)
2 Greece (1890)
3 Romania (1890)
4 Norway (1890)
5 Portugal (1890)
6 Chile (1908)
7 Brazil (1890)
8 Mexico (1900)
9 Argentina (1910)
10 China (1880)
11 China (1900)
12 China (1910)
13 Japan (1880)
14 Japan (1904)

9 The First World War

On the 2 August 1914 Germany sent an ultimatum to neutral Belgium demanding that she allow free passage for German troops in order to forestall a French attack: if they refused, war would be declared.

This blackmail did not impress King Albert and, on 4 August, he declared before both Houses of Parliament his resolution to defend Belgian territory against violation: "A country that defends itself commands universal respect: that country will never perish."

On the same day German troops marched into Belgium. In the evening the British Ambassador in Berlin delivered to Chancellor Bethmann-Hollweg his country's declaration of war against Germany in accordance with the agreements that Britain had made to guarantee the neutrality of Belgium. The Chancellor's famous and cynical remark: "*Fur einen Fetzen papier*" (all for a scrap of paper) showed clearly that he had failed to appreciate Britain's attitude in the matter, and also his total disregard for the sanctity of treaties.

The invasion of little Belgium aroused the indignation of the British public, and large numbers of volunteers appeared at the recruiting offices.

In France, the declaration of war on 3 August by the Germans (on the pretext that the French had bombarded German towns from the air) brought about the "sacred union" against their "hereditary enemy": the arrogant victor of 1871 and the despoiler of Alsace and Lorraine. The mobilisation order was posted; it was the famous white placard decorated with two French flags, and it evoked a magnificent and unanimous expression of patriotic feeling. The order was extended to foreigners living in France, and they enlisted in thousands in the course of a few days.

This was very different from the disorder of 1870, and mobilisation was effected without a hitch, although this time 3,000,000 men in 25 classes were called up. Everyone expected that the war would soon be over, the more so since the Russian "steam roller" was all set to attack the Central Powers from the rear.

FIRST WORLD WAR – FRANCE 1914

1 Chasseur à pied
2, 3 Line infantry
4 Cuirassier with breast-plate and helmet covered with material to prevent glinting in the sun
5 Dragoon
6 Senegalese
7 Marine infantry
8 Chasseur alpine

In Germany, the entire population rallied round to support the Emperor, who had promised them such a rosy future. Only the Austro-Hungarians sounded a discordant note.

On Sunday 2 August 1914 the eve of the declaration of war by Germany on France, the first two victims of the First World War met their fate. A French patrol surprised a German cavalry patrol in French territory, and the Germans under Lieutenant Meyer opened fire. Although mortally wounded, a French corporal, Andre Peugéot, slew his attacker.

Two days later the 43,000 men of the Belgium army stove to stem the first waves of the German invasion. The enemy, who had called up 4,000,000 conscripts, had 2,000,000 combatants armed with the Mauser rifle. There were 12 machine guns per regiment. Their artillery was modern and had a total of 12,000 guns. It was a formidable weapon, but it had the disadvantage of having to fight on two fronts. The French army with 1,865,000 men could muster only 4,300 guns, mostly obsolete, six machine-guns per regiment, and the Lebel rifle,

which was inferior to the Mauser. Apart from the valuable support of their formidable fleet, the British could contribute only a contingent of less than 100,000 professional soldiers.

The German plan of campaign formulated by Count Schlieffen in 1905 was based on an attack in strength through Belgium, followed by the encirclement of the French army which would then be destroyed on the frontiers of the Jura and Switzerland.

The French attacked the German frontier in force, from 7–10 August, in the direction of Sarrebruck, without making any great impression on the enemy.

Meantime, the threat from the north was increasing; despite the heroic resistance of the Belgians. The forts in Liege with their old bastions helped to stem the advance of the invaders: they contained a large part of the German army for 79 hours, giving the French army time to check the assault against Charleroi. The British Expeditionary Force arrived at last. They fought one of the most glorious battles in the history of the British army at Mons, and

FIRST WORLD WAR – FRANCE 1916–1918

1 Hussar
2 Spahi
3 Dragoon
4 Bomber
5 Machine-gunner
6 Infantry of the Line
7 Trailleur indochinois
8 Colonial infantry
9 North African infantry
10 Engineer
11 North African Infantry
12 Marine

broke the momentum of the German thrust into France.

On 25 August, Joffre deployed his troops on the Marne between Paris and Verdun, the position that had to be held at all costs.

Von Kluck, thinking that victory was already his, was surprised at the reaction of the Allied troops. Although, exhausted by a retreat lasting ten days, they still fought with unexpected determination.

An attack launched by Gallieni against the Germans with 7,000 soldiers brought to the front in Paris taxi-cabs, forced Von Kluck to withdraw troops from his centre, where the French were able to break through.

On 11 September 1914, the battle of the Marne was won. The Germans fell back and dug trenches protected with a forest of barbed wire.

On the eastern front, the Germans had been more fortunate, thanks to the efforts of Hindenburg and Ludendorff, who had destroyed a Russian army from the south, and on 31 August had gained the spectacular victory of Tannenberg, in East Prussia.

The Austrians had meanwhile been beaten at Lemberg, and the German High Command had been obliged to send reinforcements.

The German once again took up the offensive in the West, driving towards the Channel, with the object of seizing the ports of Antwerp, Calais, and Dunkirk. Antwerp held out until 10 October under very heavy bombardment, when the Belgian army was forced to retreat to the Yser. There they attacked the enemy with the help of the Allies. The threat of encirclement had been removed, and the front had been stabilised on a line from the Channel coast to the Swiss frontier. Seven hundred kilometres of trenches with ramparts of sandbags, were dug in zigzags to prevent infilading, and in and behind these 4,000,000 men marked time for the next four years.

Turkey threw in her lot with the Central Powers, and threatened Russia in the Balkans. A joint

THE GERMAN ARMY IN 1914
1 Officer
2 Infantryman
3 Hussar
4 Dragoon
5 Uhlan
6, 7 Infantryman

Franco-British naval operation launched in the Dardanelles in March 1915 failed in the face of the determined Turkish defence at Gallipoli. The Turks lost 200,000 men but forced the Allies to take once more to their ships after nine months of obstinate fighting.

The Russians soon felt the back lash of this reverse, and were forced to withdraw, losing Warsaw and Brest-Litovsk. Serbia was invaded, and the Bulgarians joined the Central Powers.

With the threat to their rear removed, the German High Command now turned its attention to the Western Front, where the Allies were strengthening their position daily.

In the Trenches, the French soldier became the *poilu*, devoting much of his ingenuity to making existence bearable. The British soldier, or "Tommy", likewise accustomed himself to the war, which he no longer looked on as a crusade. "Fritz" had the same problems, and the German soldiers fought over pieces of bread like hungry rats.

The Adrian helmet was adopted in some French units. The red trousers and greatcoats of 1914 had disappeared, and were replaced by the horizon-blue uniform, which only came into general use in 1916. All along the line, attempts were made to break through, but every time the attacks were repulsed, and every time there were dreadful casualties. A German attack on the Yser in the spring of 1915 was supported by the new and terrifying weapon (yperite) poison gas, revealing the German callousness in waging "total war". Italy joined the Allies in 1915, and an offensive in the South Tyrol and Isonzo forced the Central Powers to divert troops that were urgently needed elsewhere.

The failure of the expedition to the Dardanelles encouraged the General-in-Chief, Joffre, to launch a large-scale offensive in Champagne in the winter of 1915. This produced poor results for the loss of 300,000 men. Von Falkenhayn retaliated on 21 February 1916 with a violent attack on Verdun, the sector which he considered most vulnerable.

THE GERMAN ARMY 1915–1918

1 Dragoon (1916)
2 Uhlan of the Macedonian front
3 Infantry
4 Grenadier
5, 5a Infantry of the Line, Austrian Mountain Infantry
6 Infantryman with a gas mask
7 Palestinian infantry
8 Infantry of the Macedonian Front

1

2

3

4

5-5a

6

7

8

Throwing in the reserves, the Germans High Command assembled the troops in what were virtually underground barracks in front of the Allied lines. On the morning of 21 February 1916 a barrage from 1,000 guns along a front of 15 kilometres opened up, and lasted for nine hours, during which the men crouching in the trenches suffered terrible losses. Nevertheless they held their ground, knowing that the infantry would attack as soon as the bombardment lifted.

These brave French soldiers waited impatiently in their battered trenches for their own artillery to reply, but no shot was fired. The artillery had been cut off from the front line by the destruction of their telephone lines, and they too were subjected to this deluge of fire and iron from the Germans. Their 270 obsolete guns could not aim because of clouds of smoke caused by the bombardment. They eventually had to use runners – volunteers who dashed from shell hole to shell hole, risking death every minute and often meeting it – with orders to every part of the threatened sector.

One new weapon made its appearance: the aeroplane. However, the few French reconnaissance aircraft that went into action were driven back by the German fighters who were the masters of the sky at Verdun.

Hearing this news, Joffre hesitated to send reinforcements to Verdun, fearing that it might be a trap by the enemy and that they would attack either the area from which he had withdrawn the reinforcements for Verdun, or elsewhere!

At three o'clock in the afternoon the waves of German troops advanced behind the barrage. The French front lines was crossed without difficulty, for resistance had practically ceased. The bombardment was so heavy that in many places the French defence works were obliterated.

The French were forced to withdraw with the loss of a considerable part of the shell-torn ground. It was now that the man appeared who was to restore the situation – Philippe Petain. He organised the famous "Sacred Road" and kept up a regular flow of munitions and fresh troops, with a shuttle service

THE BELGIAN ARMY 1914–1918

1 Grenadier (1914)
2 Carabinier (1914)
3 Cyclist (1914)
4 Infantry of the Line (1914)
5 Guide (1914)
6 Minerva motor machine-gun
7, 8, 10 Infantry (1916–1918)
9 Lancer (1918)

of 3,500 lorries. On 5 March the Germans renewed the attack on Verdun and recovered some lost ground only to lose it again. In June the situation was still unchanged despite Von Falkenhayn's having fired 110,000 gas shells. The French loss reached 370,000 men.

About this time, the St Ettienne machine-gun, a good weapon but liable to jam in the dust and mud of the trenches, was replaced by the Hotchkiss heavy machine-gun.

On the following day in the north, Joffre started the preliminary bombardment for a counter-attack on the Somme, and this immediately relieved Verdun, where the enemy relaxed their pressure.

On 1 July the Allied infantry launched an attack on the enemy lines, but the Germans, forewarned by the customary bombardment, were ready for them. The infantrymen hurled themselves against the barbed wire which the artillery bombardment had been supposed to destroy; the impetus of the assault was checked as the men tried to find a way through the wire. Then the German machine-guns opened up and mowed down the attacking infantry, but wave upon wave of Allied troops persevered until eventually they reached their objective. The losses were out of all proportion to the ground gained; the British alone lost 19,000 killed and 38,000 wounded. The battle lasted several days, gradually exhausting the Allied reserves without breaking the German front, where defences stretched back in some places for as much as 45 kilometres.

On 14 September the British troops received relief. Their reinforcements arrived, and a constant flow of troops was henceforth assured by the introduction of compulsory military service. The tiny expeditionary force of 1914 had become a powerful army.

At dawn on 15 September a new weapon appeared to lead the British attack: the tank. This formidable machine, armed with guns and machine-guns, had a considerable psychological effect on the German soldiers who saw it rise up out of the early morning mist, rumbling and rolling, impervious to the fire of the Spandau machine-guns.

BRITISH ARMY BEFORE 1914
1 Life Guards
2 Private, Rifle Brigade
3 5th Lancers
4 Private, Coldstream Guards
5 Private, Gordon Highlanders

1

2

3

4

5

Many of the Germans were so terrified that they fled. Others stood their ground bravely in a hopeless attempt to stop this monster which crushed their barbed wire and crossed over the trenches.

Soon, however, the German artillery replied with their quick-firing guns, and shells rained down on the 32 British tanks. All the same, the results were excellent. The infantry had penetrated deep into the enemy lines at a number of points. The advantage was, it is true, nullified by the absence of reserves to consolidate the ground gained. The British High Command was responsible, for they had had little real faith in the new weapon.

In the weeks that followed, the tank continued to support the infantry with varying degrees of success, depending on how it was used. And as fast as the British made improvements to the tank and its basic design, the Germans tried to devise ways of destroying it.

The Battle of the Somme ended in December, without any real gains. On the other hand, this offensive had shaken the morale of the German army and had put 550,000 troops out of action.

With material support from the Allies, the Russians had resumed the offensive on the Eastern front and had broken through the Austrian lines.

After some heart-searching on the part of her sovereign, Ferdinand I, who was a Hohenzollern by birth, Romania joined the Allies. By this sacrifice on behalf of his people, King Ferdinand escaped the fate which befell the family of the German emperor.

Between 24 October and 2 November, the French re-took the forts of Douaumont and Vaux, making Verdun once again the focal point of the war. Ten months of bitter fighting and one million dead ended with the defeat of the Germans. But although the legend of the invincibility of the German army had been destroyed at Verdun, the tide had not yet turned.

The sinking of the *Lusitania*[1] on 7 May 1915, under the policy of total submarine warfare ordered by Hindenburg and Ludendorff, coming on top of the

1 British liner; there were a number of Americans aboard.

BRITISH ARMY 1914–1918
1 Colonial Infantry
2 Cavalry
3 Bengal Lancer
4 Canadian Infantry
5 Infantry (1914)
6, 7, 8 Infantry (1916–18)
9 Scots Infantry

German interference in the quarrel between Mexico and the United States, made President Wilson decide to come in on the side of the Allies. On 2 April 1917, the United States declared war.

On 16 April a heavy attack by the French opened the first phase of a big Allied offensive. The French used tanks for the first time: 400 Schneiders and Saint-Chamonds. After three days of bitter fighting and the loss of 60,000 men, the French failed to break the enemy lines, and the world was left to remember the tragedy of the *Chemin des Dames*.

The continued heavy casualties inevitably led to defeatism, and some units of the French army mutinied. But Petain, with his deep understanding of the psychology of the fighting man, managed to avert the crisis by making one or two examples.

In Russia, the successful offensive of Broussilov in June 1917 was reversed when Russia's new Bolshevik leaders concluded a separate armistice with the Germans.

The Austro-German armies could now be moved from the Eastern Front to Italy where they won the resounding victory of Caporetto, capturing 265,000 prisoners and a vast quantity of arms, including 3,000 guns.

In the meantime Greece had come in on the side of the Allies, and Turkey had lost Baghdad and Jerusalem, but these successes did not compensate setbacks elsewhere.

In France, the British offensive in Flanders in July produced excellent results, and the French had at last retaken the *Chemin des Dames*. The enemy front, however, was still intact.

In January 1918 the German High Command decided to launch what they hoped would be the final offensive on the Western Front and began to bring up troops and to reinforce the artillery. The attack was launched on 21 March 1918 and was supported by 6,200 guns; it brought an initial success over the British army, which was forced to fall back some 30 kilometres despite all resistance. This resulted in a gap between the British and the French armies, and Petain threw in twenty divisions to fill it.

1914–1918 WAR–OTHER ARMIES (I)

1, 2 Turkish infantry
3 Turkish officer
4 Bulgarian officer
5 Bulgarian infantry
6, 7 Russian infantry
8 Russian cavalry
9 Cossack
10 Siberian infantry

Realising the dangers of operating under two commands, the Allies decided to place their forces under the single command of Foch, who was appointed Generalissimo. And it was not before time! Already Paris was being shelled by long-range guns from a distance of 120 kilometres.

The German impetus was checked, but Ludendorff, determined on victory at any price, returned to the charge on 14 April, but again failed to break through. All he got were two little pockets of ground, dangerously exposed.

Obstinately pursuing his plan of campaign, on 27 May Ludendorff again attacked the *Chemin des Dames*. The French had withdrawn troops to the north and the Germans now had a numerical superiority of three to one. The 30 divisions under the Crown Prince overran the British and French armies' positions, reached Soissons on 29 May, and were soon at the Marne. Paris was threatened, as it had been in 1870. Foch however did not lose his nerve. The German success, though remarkable, was only tactical; it was not a strategic victory.

All available forces were committed in this battle, among them the first American troops to fight in the war. The Germans were finally halted 70 kilometres from Paris.

Two days later, with like determination, the Austro-Hungarians broke the Italian lines, and it took a week's bitter fighting to halt them on the Piave.

Ludendorff's final effort started on 15 July 1918, but the Allies were prepared and the assaults were repulsed. By nightfall the offensive was broken, and on 18 July the Germans fell back on Château-Thierry. The Americans, with 1,200,000 men now in France, played a brilliant part in this action. At the same time, a force of 480 Renault tanks retook Soissons.

The time had come for Foch to launch a general offensive. The Allied armies attacked on 8 August with strong artillery support. The German pockets of resistance were neutralised and then, on 26 September, the Allies attacked in strength all along the front.

1914–1918 WAR – OTHER ARMIES (II)

1 Serbia
2 Romania
3 Montenegro
4 Greece
5, 6 U.S.A.
7 Poland
8 Italy
9 Italian Bersagliere
10 Japan

This was the beginning of the end for the Central Powers who now found themselves everywhere forced on to the defensive. In Syria and Mesopotamia the Turks were defeated, the Bulgarians were driven back on the Salonica front, and in German East Africa the fighting was nearly over.

The German people began to realise the futility of the sacrifices that their Emperor had called upon them to make. Now practically starving, they were sick of seeing youths of 18 sent to the slaughter.

Between August and October 1918, the Allies broke the German front by successive attacks. France and Belgium were liberated after a series of battles against a German army which, though retreating, still fought with determination. In four months, more than a million Allied soldiers paid with their lives in this final struggle for victory.

In Germany, the grumbling of revolution could be heard: the revolt started with a mutiny in the fleet at Keil, where the sailors refused to put to sea to attack the Royal Navy. Workers and soldiers in the principal towns in Germany rose in revolt, and Kaiser William II fled to Holland.

In the meantime Turkey had surrendered, and Austria-Hungary, under heavy attack by the Italians, decided that it was useless to continue the now hopeless struggle.

What the great Lyautey had called in 1914 "the most monumental piece of stupidity the world has ever known" ended with a final total of eight million dead. France alone had lost 1,457,000 men, the British Empire 1,000,000, Russia 1,700,000, and Germany, Austria and Hungary between them counted three million men dead. These horrifying figures did not include the wounded, the mutilated, and the crippled, of whom there were almost twice that number.

AIRCRAFT AND ARMOURED FIGHTING VEHICLES, 1914–1918

1 British gun
2 French 75mm gun
3 305 Austrian gun
4 German gun
5 French Voisin bomber (1916)
6 French Spad fighter
7 German Aviatak
8 British Handley-Page bomber (1917)
9 English Sopwith Camel fighter
10 French Nieuport fighter
11 British tank (1916)
12 German tank (1918)
13 French Saint-Chamond tank
14 French Schneider tank
15 French Renault tank

10 *The Second World War*

On 28 June 1919 the Germans signed the Treaty of Versailles in the same Hall of Mirrors that had seen the coronation of their first Emperor. The terms had been harsh, but were nevertheless largely justified by the results of the policy of total war for which the Kaiser had been responsible. From now on the German army was not permitted to exceed 100,000 men, compulsory military service was forbidden, aircraft and tanks were prohibited, and the Navy was to be limited to 18 warships.

The reparations, fixed in 1921 at the enormous sum of 138,000,000,000 gold marks, were to be payable at the rate of 2,000,000,000 gold marks a year.

Unable to pay her debts, and the victim of inflation and unemployment, Germany asked for a moratorium. France and Belgium then occupied the Ruhr Valley, as a means of guaranteeing payment. This angered the German people, and they retaliated with strikes and riots fomented by nationalist secret societies.

The Pact of Locarno relieved tension a little, and the German debt was reduced to 116,000,000,000 marks and then to 3,000,000,000 marks but none of it was ever paid.

The memory of the terrible war years persuaded governments to pursue a policy of peace and appeasement at any price, and the authoritarian regimes in Europe were quick to profit from this.

Italy had emerged victorious from the war, but nonetheless was undergoing a serious economic crisis: revolution was in the air. The fascist movement found its firmest foothold among the middle classes. Its leader, Benito Mussolini, gathered together his adherents, mostly old soldiers, in *Fascio di combattimento*, from which the words fascist and fascism are derived. These fascists wore a uniform with a black shirt, which left their aggressive intentions in little doubt. Mussolini was nicknamed *Il Duce* (leader) and he soon embarked upon his "politics of action" which replaced the democratic regime which was considered rotten.

In Germany, Adolf Hitler also created an entirely new party, the N.S.D.A.P. (National-Socialist German Workers Party), and was elected as its president with the full support of the *Reichswehr* (the German Army), a pact that the German generals were later bitterly to regret.

1939–1945 WAR – GERMAN AND ITALIAN ARMIES

1, 2 German infantry
3 German Air Force: ground-defence troops
4, 5 German parachute troops
6 German anti-tank gun and crew
7 Soldier of the Afrika Korps
8 German General Officer
9 Italian infantry
10 German cavalry

Hitler's primary objective was to raise an unbeatable army, while all along proclaiming the peaceful intentions of the Third Reich.

Compulsory military service was reinstated and the army brought up to a strength of 600,000 in defiance of the Treaty of Versailles. The fleet was enlarged by agreement with Britain who, without due consideration, accorded Germany the right to a fleet equivalent to 35 per cent of the tonnage of the Royal Navy.

The memory of the part that armoured fighting-vehicles played in the last Allied offensive in 1918 was not forgotten; the German army built up armoured divisions and motorised units to replace the outdated cavalry.

The tanks which would, sooner or later, confront the armoured fighting-vehicles of the victors of the First World War, were fitted with heavier armour-plate which would stand up to enemy infantry fire.

In 1935 the Panzer divisions each comprised two tank regiments, one infantry regiment, one motorised artillery regiment, one engineer battalion, one signal battalion, one motor-cycle battalion, one anti-tank company, and a unit of light anti-aircraft guns (the D.C.A.).

The German Air Force, the *Luftwaffe*, was also resuscitated. This was equipped with specially developed aircraft to outclass the air forces of the various signatories of the Treaty of Versailles, now that the Germans were ignoring it as a dead letter.

While Hitler was preparing his revenge, Mussolini attacked Ethiopia after an incident at Walwal, where an Italian force broke up an Ethiopian detachment. An accusation of violating the frontiers was brought before the League of Nations which temporised, fearing to offend Mussolini, and considering that the Emperor Haile Selassie should submit to Italy's demands in the cause of peace.

On 3 October 1935 the Fascist troops invaded Ethiopia with 320,000 men supported by tanks and 300 aircraft. The Ethiopians, poorly armed, made mistake of trying to resist the invasion with a *levée en masse*. They were driven back, lost Adowa, and the Italians took up a position along the Takkaze. Having reformed their forces, the Ethiopians launched a counter-attack with startling success,

GERMANY 1939–1945
1 Stuka
2 Focke-Wulf 190
3 V-1 Flying Bomb
4 Messerschmitt 109
5 Dornier 217
6 Junker 88
7 Panzer III tank
8 Panther anti-tank gun
9 Tiger tank
10 Flame thrower (recoilless gun)
11 Recoilless anti-tank gun

...

119

so much so that the big military depot at Adi Quala was threatened. The Fascist Command realised that they were in danger of losing the battle, and decided to use a more powerful argument: several squadrons of aircraft took off and dropped mustard-gas bombs, which had the expected results. The experiment was repeated twice in January 1936 and did much to restore the situation for the Italians.

From now on, the Ethiopian Army suffered successive defeats. They made a final effort on 1 April. Having gained the advantage during the first two days of the battle, the troops of Haile Selassie were attacked by the Italians with mustard gas while they were sleeping; they awoke and fled for their lives, and by May 1936 Mussolini was master of Ethiopia.

But the Italian Army was already becoming divided within itself. The fascist Black-Shirt units had been incorporated into the army and were under the command of fanatical and totally incompetent militants. This gradually aroused the antagonism of the regular army.

Realising his precarious position in Ethiopia, Mussolini tried to consolidate his *impero* by forming the famous Rome-Berlin Axis with Hitler.

The Spanish War broke out on 17 July 1936. It proved to be a dress-rehearsal for the Second World War and a testing ground for the totalitarian powers.

The new German motorised artillery had its first trials in Spain. The waves of Heinkels and of the Savoia-Marchetti inscribed the first names on the rolls of honour of the martyred towns.

Like fascist Italy, Japan had broken with her former allies and in 1937 she embarked upon the invasion of China. The war that was thus started dragged on for eight years.

In Europe, the Western powers tried in vain to control the Fuhrer's belligerent activities. Hitler reoccupied the Rhine and constructed the Siegfried line. He annexed Austria and soon was casting covetous eyes on Czechoslovakia and her valuable Skoda armaments factories.

Under the pretext of protecting the German minority in Sudetenland, Hitler invaded Czechoslovakia, loudly proclaiming that this was positively his last territorial demand. Mussolini for his part occupied Albania.

The Führer was now set to put into effect his secret

FRANCE 1939–1940
1 Infantry, winter dress
2 Garrison troops
3 Cavalry
4 Field service marching order
5 Morane fighter
6 Curtiss fighter
7 Armoured car equipped with radio
8 Light reconnaissance tank
9 "B" tank
10 Anti-tank gun

plans for world domination, and he turned upon Poland as a preliminary to confronting the Western Powers.

Secure behind the Siegfried Line, and reassured by the strictly defensive attitude adopted by France and Britain, he launched his *Blitzkrieg* (lightning war) against unfortunate Poland, who had not dared to order general mobilisation lest she incurred the wrath of her irascible neighbour. Poland could muster only 750,000 men, 250 tanks and a few hundred aircraft to oppose the weight of 69 German divisions.

Cornered, the gallant Polish troops were also subjected to attack by a new aircraft, the Stuka[1], which dived almost vertically out of the sky with a siren screaming, and which dropped its bombs with remarkable accuracy. Through the gaps made by these bombardments, the 2,300 German tanks and motorised troops were able to attack the Poles, whose aircraft stood immobilised on airfields that were pitted with bomb craters.

In a few weeks the Poles were defeated. Russia, as a signatory to the German-Soviet pact, had taken the Eastern frontier. All resistance ceased on 7

October, but the Germans had paid dearly for their defeat of the Poles, for Hitler's Panzer divisions had been reduced by a quarter, and his Air Force by a half.

On 3 September 1939 Britiain and France declared war on Germany, and tried to help their ally by attacking the outposts along the Siegfried Line. After the collapse of Poland, both sides dug in, and the period known as the "phoney war" began

It was indeed a phoney war, confined to a few half-hearted artillery barrages and air raids by the Allies when leaflets were dropped. Meanwhile the British soldiers sang: "We're going to hang out our washing on the Siegfried Line . . ." The Allied desire for peace was made clear by this attitude, though it was not realised until after more than five years of bitter fighting against a determined enemy.

The Russians, for their part, anxious to strengthen their position, demanded that Finland cede part of her territory. The demand was refused, and on 30 November 1939 the Russians marched into

1 Abbreviation for Sturzkampfbombenwerfer

OTHER ARMIES 1939–1945
1 Belgian Chasseur ardennais
2 Belgian infantry (1940)
3 Belgian Guide (1940)
4 Poland (1939)
5 Czechoslovakia (1939)
6 Yugoslavian partisan (1944)
7 Finnish patrol with anti-tank gun (1944)
8 Holland (1940)
9 Russian (1939–1940)
10 Hungary (1939)

Finland. The League of Nations made a half-hearted protest, expressing sympathy for the Finnish people, and left it at that. The Finns had to face the Soviet colossus alone. The Russian force pushed its way forward painfully into deep forests in a temperature of minus 50 degrees below. Using guerrilla tactics, the Finns enjoyed considerable success. The "death patrols" travelled on skis, dressed entirely in white, and infiltrated behind the Russian lines where they did extensive damage.

The first Russian offensive failed, but in February 1940 a second attack strongly supported by artillery broke the Finnish resistance. The armistice was signed on 12 March.

This short campaign, the details of which were made known by contradictory and biased communiques, gave an unflattering and wildly inaccurate picture of the Soviet army.

The German High Command made the same mistake as well, and paid dearly for it later on.

On 9 April 1940, Hitler invaded Denmark, a formality which took less than a day. Then he turned to Norway which he knew to be a favourable spot for an Allied landing. Despite objections from his generals who considered the operation extremely hazardous, Hitler launched "Operation Weser". Concealed in apparently unarmed merchant ships, the Germans troops made a surprise landing on 9 April 1940 at several points along the Norwegian coast, supported by 1,200 aircraft. The Norwegians were able to put up only a feeble resistance and surrendered two months later.

At sea, the Germans were less successful. Early in April they lost several battleships and a number of transports carrying munitions in attacks by the Royal Navy.

An expeditionary force of British, French and Polish troops was hastily assembled and landed in Norway and the Faroes between 15 and 19 April. However, as they were without tanks, anti-tank guns or heavy artillery, they were forced to withdraw after fierce fighting in which the Foreign Legion covered itself with glory. The prestige of the Allies nevertheless suffered, and the increasingly confident Hitler put his main plan into action. This was "Operation Yellow", the invasion of France, Belgium, and Holland.

BRITISH ARMY 1939–1945
1, 2 Infantry
3 Infantry, 8th Army
4 Commando
5 Paratrooper
6 Paratroopers with machine-gun
7 Armoured Car
8 Anti-tank gun

1   2   3   4   5

6   7

8

In a final harangue to his soldiers, Hitler declared that the forthcoming struggle "would decide the fate of Germany for a thousand years to come", and then sent his fanaticised troops into the attack, just before dawn on 10 May 1940.

Three larges armies took part in the attack with 136 divisions, 2,574 tanks, and an air force three times as strong as that of the Allies, who had 149 divisions but less than 1,000 tanks.

Belgium, Holland, and Luxembourg were invaded without war being declared. While the German Air Force bombed their rear, the heavy tanks broke the front line to let the light tanks and motorised troops supported by Stukas pass through. Pockets of resistance were cut off by the advanced troops and then destroyed by the heavy formations which followed.

The Belgian fortresses were attacked by parachute troops and neutralised at once. The Germans had learned the full details of the Belgian defence works from their spies. In 1939 they had even made a model of the fortress of Eben-Emael which was believed to be impregnable, in order to decide exactly how to capture it. When the time came, the Eben-Emael fell in less than 48 hours.

On 14 May the Dutch Army surrendered after a fierce fight. Meanwhile, German tanks under von Kleist were advancing 40 to 60 kilometres a day. On 21 May, after eight days, they reached Abbeville and the French coast, splitting the Allied armies in two and cutting off the troops in Flanders.

The spectacular success of the German armour was due to the efforts of General Guderian, who had worked on the creation of this force since 1928 and had perfected the Blitzkrieg tactics.

There were four types of German tank: Panzer[1] I, II, III and IV. The Panzer I weighed 5.3 tons and dated from 1934. It carried a crew of two and two machine-guns, and had a speed of about 35 kilometres an hour. The Panzer II, dating from the end of 1934, weighed 7.5 tons, had a crew of three, one 20-mm gun and one machine-gun.

The Panzer III, designed and built in 1936, weighed

---

1 From Panzerkamfwagen

BRITISH AEROPLANES AND TANKS 1939–1945

1 Hurricane
2 Bristol Blenheim
3 Wellington
4 Halifax
5 Lancaster
6 Mosquito
7 Spitfire
8 Heavy tank (1943) Mark VIII
9 Churchill bridge-builder
10 Churchill tank Mark VII
11 Shaffy tank, 8th Army

1

2

3

4

5

6

7

8

9

10

11

15 tons, and only differed from the Panzer IV, which was 5 tons heavier, in its armament. It mounted a 50-mm gun, instead of the 75-mm gun of the Panzer IV, and they both carried a crew of five. They had the same armour. Three hundred and thirty-four Czechoslovak Škoda tanks completed the armoured force with which the German army went into battle.

Despite repeated warnings by an officer who was to become one of the greatest figures of the Second World War, Charles de Gaulle, the French Army had only four motorised divisions, acting in support of the infantry as they had done at the end of the War of 1914–18.

The idea that a continuous line could not be broken was proved false by the achievements of the German armour, which anyway out-numbered the French. Moreover, the German tanks were proof against the French 47-mm anti-tank guns.

The British, who had invented the tank, had only one Tank Division, and only a part of it had landed on the continent to support the infantry. Matilda tanks attacked Rommel's flanks on 21 May. Slow,

but heavily armoured, they withstood the German 37-mm anti-tank guns. Rommel, thanks to his quick thinking, escaped disaster. Using every available 88-mm anti-aircraft gun in an anti-tank role, he destroyed 36 British tanks and put the rest to flight.

Soon, the collapse was a *fait accompli*. Only an unhoped-for intervention by Hitler, who held back his tanks so that the infantry could catch up with them, gave the British the opportunity to extricate the 220,000 men of the British Expeditionary Force, together with the 118,000 French and Belgian soldiers also cut off at Dunkirk. These men were ferried to Britain by a fleet of 900 strangely assorted vessels, but not without the sacrifice of the French rearguard which stubbornly opposed the enemy to the end.

Now came the second part of the campaign in which the Germans had to defeat the 70 divisions of the Allies, two of them British, on the southern front.

Divided into two groups, A and B, the armoured divisions advanced for the final battle. The 7th Division under Rommel broke through the Allied

JAPAN 1944
1 Mitsubishi S-00
2 Betty 22
3 Mitsubishi C-94
4 Kawasaki Hien
5 Nakajimi
6 Torpedo bomber
7 Officer
8, 9 Infantryman
10 Soldier with helmet and Type 99 rifle
11 Armoured car
12, 13 Tanks

lines and reached Rouen on 8 June, where it outflanked a Scottish Division and a number of French troops and drove them back to the coast. Four other armoured divisions were not so successful; they were held up in the area of Amiens and at Péronne. At Rethel, further to the east, the French 14th Infantry Division under the future Marshal de Lattre de Tassigny beat off the German assault and took several hundred prisoners.

The Allies' situation was desperate, and the Germans finally broke through, despite determined resistance.

On 14 June the Maginot Line, which Hitler had left alone, up to now, became the target for the German heavy artillery and Luftwaffe. Then, under cover of smoke, and equipped with flame-throwers and explosives, the shock troops outflanked and destroyed the French fortresses one by one. By 16 June the French had been pushed back beyond the Loire. Six days earlier Mussolini had invaded the Riviera—a pointless stab in the back, as Franklin Roosevelt described the declaration of war on France by *Il Duce*, an act that earned for him only universal contempt. On 22 June 1940 a humiliating armistice was signed by the French in the same railway carriage where twenty-two years earlier Marshal Foch had dictated the terms to the Germany of Kaiser William II.

Although all seemed irremediably lost, Britain, inspired by her great Prime Minister Winston Churchill, carried on the struggle alone. Insulted, Hitler determined to invade England. His plans, however, had no firm basis as yet, so the Great Dictator gave the Luftwaffe the job of destroying his defiant enemy.

The Battle of Britain began on 10 July 1940 and reached its climax in September with the air raids on English towns.

The British fighter squadrons included many French, Belgian, Dutch and Polish pilots who distinguished themselves beside their British comrades. The Royal Air Force fought off the German attacks against all odds, and in the summer of 1941 Hitler, having lost 1,733 aircraft, realised that his Blitz had failed.

In his quest for glory, Mussolini invaded Greece on 28 October 1940. A month later he withdrew,

U.S.A. 1941–1945

1 Infantry (1941)
2 Infantry, summer dress
3 Infantry, winter dress
4 Infantry, winter dress (Bastogne)
5 Corporal, U.S. Marines
6 Parachutist
7 Bazooka and crew
8 60mm mortar and crew

defeated, to Albania, calling for help from his old ally, Hitler. At the same time, he lost his newly won Ethiopian Empire, which led to the Afrika Korps under Rommel intervening in Libya. However, the Fascist powers were not beaten yet: Yugoslavia, hesitant at accepting the German offers of an alliance, had a taste of the Blitzkrieg along with Greece, and in Africa the British were driven back to Egypt.

Hitler could see that his "lightning war" was hanging fire, and decided to settle with the "pig-headed" British later. To deal with them, he would require enormous material resources, and Soviet Russia had what he wanted. If he destroyed the "colossus with feet of clay", he would have all the riches he desired and at the same time safeguard his war.

On the night of 21–22 June 1941, three army groups were poised ready for a campaign that Hitler believed would last only two or three months. The plan was simple: the Northern Army under van Leeb would destroy the Russian Baltic armies and take Leningrad: the Central Army under von Bock would march against Smolensk and Moscow, and the Southern Army under von Rundstedt would deal with the enemy in the Ukraine and take Kiev or Kharkov.

To effect this glorious conquest, Germany assembled 121 divisions, 17 armoured and 12 motorised, in all some 3,000,000 men with 3,200 tanks, and 2,740 aircraft, these last gathered with some difficulty after the heavy losses in the Battle of Britain.

Heavy artillery fire and extensive aerial bombardment opened the way for the armoured divisions which went in to the attack at a quarter past four on the morning of 22 June. The Russians were taken by surprise and withdrew in disorder with the loss of 1,200 aircraft, most of which were destroyed on the ground. It is hard to believe that Germany and the Soviet Union had signed a pact of non-aggression only twenty-two months earlier.

The Russian tanks tried courageously to stem the flood of the Nazi armour, but were destroyed. These tanks were models BT-5, BT-7 and T-26, and all three had inadequate armour and armament.

Hundreds of thousands of Russians were taken prisoner, and the Führer's prophecies appeared to be coming true.

U.S.A. ARMOURED CORPS AND AIR FORCE

1 Stuart tank
2 Sherman tank in the French army
3 Rocket tank
4 Corsair
5 Lightning
6 Liberator
7 Mustang
8 Flying Fortress
9 Thunderbolt
10 Wildcat
11 105mm howitzer
12 Mine-sweeping tank
13 105mm self-propelled howitzer

1
2
3

4
5
6
7
8
9
10

11
12
13

In July a new type of Russian tank appeared discreetly, and surprised the Germans both by its speed and its resistance to anti-tank fire. It was the 28-ton T-34.

Nevertheless, the German advance continued, though without effecting the long-heralded defeat of the Russian Army. The Russians were retreating but behind them they left only desolation, the result of their "scorched earth" policy. The German lines of communication became longer and longer, which made them an easy prey for the numerous groups of partisans.

The winter of 1941–42 was very severe. The Russians counter-attacked with 100 divisions, and the Germans, paralysed by the cold, in temperatures below minus 40 degrees, halted in sight of Moscow.

Although the Russians had lost hundreds of thousands of men, they refused to be driven on to the defensive. In the autumn, new types of heavy tank appeared and these inflicted heavy casualties on the German armies under von Bock and Guderian. There was the brand new 46-ton KV-1 tank which, despite its weight, had a speed of 40 kilometres an hour, as fast as the 23-ton Panzer IV, and it carried heavier armour and a more powerful gun. There was also the T-34 medium tank which, with a speed of nearly 50 kilometres an hour plus its gun and its armour, was superior to any of the enemy tanks. The Germans, too, were working on a new tank that could stand up to the dangerous newcomer.

As they waited, the terrible cold of the winter put the German army and its equipment severely to the test. Radiators froze, and automatic weapons jammed. A vigorous Russian counter-attack pushed the enemy back between 60 and 70 kilometres, and showed the inadequacy of Adolf Hitler's private brand of strategy.

The following summer, the Führer changed his objective and turned towards the Caucasus and the petrol there, which was desperately needed by both sides.

For their part, the Russians had spent the winter feverishly assembling new armies built round a nucleus of powerful armoured and motorised corps and artillery regiments with heavy tanks. The German change of objective caught the Russians unawares, and at the end of August the Army of the

U.S.S.R. 1941–1945

1 Soldier
2 Officer
3 Winter uniform
4 Commando
5 Soldier with 50mm mortar
6 120mm mortar
7, 8 Summer dress
9 Tank corps, winter uniform
10 Siberian infantry with Degtyarev anti-tank rifle

Caucasus reached Terek and Stalingrad. This produced positive results and Hitler ordered von Paulus to hold Stalingrad, the city that was named after his deadly enemy; strange obtuseness that resulted in General Chuykov's surrounding some 300,000 exhausted German troops. For two terrible months the Germans tried to break out, but were finally forced to surrender on 21 January 1943 with the loss of two-thirds of their effective force.

Coupled with the defeats in Africa, the fall of Stalingrad shook the confidence of the German people in their leader, but Hitler lost none of his conceit and continued blindly along the road to destruction.

The tide was turning everywhere. In Africa, Rommel and the Afrika Korps, after their earlier successes, had been defeated at El Alamein by General Montgomery. The United States had entered the war, bringing all her resources in materials and manpower. The war at sea, where for some time the German Navy had had the upper hand, was turned against them. Furthermore, Italy, having shaken off the yoke of her dictator, had signed an armistice in September 1943.

In the war in the air too, fortunes changed. The Luftwaffe, dispersed over several theatres of operations, was subjected to increasingly severe air raids by the Allies, sometimes with up to 1,300 aircraft. Bombing raids cost the Third Reich nearly 500,000 dead, and destroyed an enormous number of buildings. Now Hitler was reaping what he had sown.

By the spring of 1944 the German armies in the East were retreating slowly but surely before the now superior Soviet army.

The Allied assault against the "Fortress of Europe" caught Hitler in a vice. On "D Day"—6 June 1944—the most powerful armada in history sailed from the coast of England for France. The Atlantic Wall was breached, but it was two months after the bridgehead had been established that the first breakthrough by the Sherman and Churchill tanks was made.

After bitter fighting the American armour under under Patton broke through the German defences and fanned out into Normandy and Brittany. The British broke through at Argentan and Falaise,

U.S.S.R. ARMOURED CORPS AND AIR FORCE 1940–1945

1 Lagg-3
2 Jak-1
3 1-16 RATA
4 Mig-1
5 1-153
6 DB-3
7 SU-122 tank
8 SU-76 tank
9 T-34 tank
10 Heavy machine-gun
11 Simonov anti-tank rifle

Paris was liberated on 25 August 1944 by the French armour, under Leclerc, which had distinguished itself at Tchad, in Libya and in Tunisia alongside the British and the Americans. A second landing was made, this time in the south of France, and the force advanced without great difficulty to join up with the armies of the north, while the French Forces of the Interior harassed the enemy's rear.

Hitler's Germany seemed near to defeat, but his troops made a last desperate stand in the Belgian Ardennes, where the Americans distinguished themselves at Bastogne.

Retreating on all fronts, the remnants of the German army fought desperately to the last, but finally capitulated on 7 May 1945.

The war continued, however, in the Far East where the Americans, who had hitherto given priority to Europe, turned to deal with the Japanese aggressor.

Between 1943 and 1944 they had re-taken one after another of the Pacific Islands occupied by the Japanese. The fight for Tarawa symbolised the bitterness of the struggle between the U.S. Marines and the fanatical Japanese. The offensive against the Philippines in October 1944 sounded the death knell of the Japanese Imperial Navy which was defeated by the U.S. Navy.

After this, there followed the final battles for the Islands of Iwo-Jima and Okinawa. The suicidal Japanese resistance reached its height, and they lost 123,000 out of 131,000 men.

No longer hopeful of unconditional surrender by Japan, the President of the United States, Harry S. Truman, authorised the dropping of the first atomic bomb on Hiroshima on 6 August 1945, and a second on Nagasaki on 9 August. The following day the Japanese sued for peace.

Although no precise reckoning has been made, it seems certain that the material cost of World War II exceeded that of the rest of the wars in history put together. The total number of fatalities, including those killed in battle and civilians of all countries, is estimated to have been close on 55 million.

1939–1945 WAR

1 Macchi C-22 (Italy)
2 Romeo (Italy)
3 Savoia S-79 (Italy)
4 Macchi C-202 (Italy)
5 Fiat BR-20 (Italy)
6 Alpine artillery (Italy)
7 Bersagliere, tropical dress (Italy)
8 Chinese infantry
9 Free French soldier
10 Russian Tokarev rifle
11 American Garand rifle
12 British MK1 No 4 rifle
13 German model 43 rifle

139

In the first days of the Second World War a young pilot called Rene Duvauchelle (Companion of the Liberation and an R.A.F. hero, who was killed on 11 January 1941) wrote: "Where will Europe end up at this rate? An aged Europe worn out and too small, full of extravagant ideas. Are we to pay for the excesses of civilisation and general selfishness? That all this were leading to a return of faith, a love for generosity!" But the hoped-for dawn did not come.

No sooner was the Japanese threat got rid of, than China became the centre of the struggle between Chiang Kai-chek supported by the United States, and Mao Tse-Tung's communist bands, supported by Russia. Hostilities in China ended in 1949 with a victory for Mao, but war broke out again in Korea in 1950. Numerous European contingents fought alongside the Americans who formed the principal force, in a land that no one wanted. Britain sent one brigade, France and Belgium each sent a battalion known as the "Korea Battalions" who fought gallantly. This war which nearly ended in disaster cost the United Nations forces 157,000 dead, of whom 142,000 were American. Again, tanks played a major part in the conflict, notably those of the American 1st Cavalry Division.

Although the atomic era had opened so tragically with the great mushrooms over Hiroshima and Nagasaki, in the wars that followed conventional arms, developed between 1939 and 1945 and later perfected, were used.

Rockets, which had not been seen for more than a century, had reappeared greatly improved in the form of the German reprisal weapons, the VI and the V2 in 1944.

The famous 'Stalin's Organs' firing salvos of small rockets had been copied and improved by the Germans, and later by the Americans. Even smaller rockets were developed that could be fired by one man; an example is the famous American bazooka.

The old struggle between armour and armament was renewed. In order to counter the T-34s with their quick-firing guns, the Germans had developed the Panther and Tiger tanks weighing 45 and 56 tons, with increasingly thick armour.

The new British Centurion tank, which dated from 1945, was not engaged in the final phases of the Second World War. The Korean War provided the opportunity for it to show its paces. Weighing 50 tons and with a crew of four, the Centurion had

MODERN ARMIES (I)

1 Denmark
2 Italy
3 West Germany
4 Belgium
5 Holland
6 East Germany
7 Vietcong with collar for carrying rice
8 Belgian F.N. "Fal" rifle
9 Italian Beretta submachine gun
10 Belgian Vigneron submachine gun
11 French short-range radar
12 Jeep with recoilless gun (France)
13 AMX bridge-layer (France)

automatic stabilisers which prevent the gun, after it has been laid, from firing before the tank is on an even keel.

The Mark II Centurions proved their value during the Korean War. Since then, the Centurion Mark III has become accepted as one of the best tanks in the world. It is armed with a 105-mm gun and it has been adopted by many armies both in Europe and elsewhere.

After the Second World War, the American Army had adopted the 30-ton Sherman armed with a 76-mm gun. The tank was replaced by the Patton or M-46 which took part in the Korean War where various defects became obvious. It was replaced in 1951 by the M-47, which was faster than the others, and is now used by many countries including France, Belgium, and Italy.

The French armoured forces, equipped at the end of the war with American tanks, designed a tank of their own in 1946, the AMX50. This was replaced by the improved AMX13 which was both lighter and better designed, and went into production in 1952. The AMX13 had a speed of 65 kilometres an hour, was armed with a 75-mm quick-firing gun, and had a crew of three. This tank aroused general interest, and several nations placed orders for it.

The Russians had also made progress and had brought into service the T-44, an improved version of the T-34-85. Then, in 1950, they produced the 36-ton T-54, armed with a 100-mm gun and with a speed of 55 kilometres an hour.

Small arms and automatic weapons made enormous progress during the Second World War, and most of them remained in use for some time to come, some up to the present day.

Modern arms give the soldier a fire-power twenty times that of 1914, and one hundred times that of the rifleman at the end of the last century.

The Korean War was barely over when the world's attention was drawn to another field of operations: Indochina, where a French army of 500,000, of whom 225,000 were from Laos, Vietnam and Cambodia, was struggling against an army raised by the Vietminh which was well versed in the type of war being waged. This war was different, quite unlike the classic war.

The Vietminh army was composed of four distinct categories of soldier:
1) peasants, who were used as porters and men of all work;
2) guerrillas, who were snipers, working by day and harassing the enemy by night;

MODERN ARMIES (II)
1 French MAS submachine-gun
2 7.5mm French machine-gun on tripod
3 French M1949/56 rifle
4 U.S.A. Artillery Officer (Korea)
5 British Paratrooper
6 French infantryman in campaign uniform
7 French officer in full dress
8 British version of the F.N. automatic
9 American M.16 with telescopic sight

3) local levies organised in companies; and
4) regular soldiers wearing uniform, and equipped by communist China.

Despite the efforts of the French, the situation worsened year by year, though in the summer of 1953 the French had some undoubted successes.

The Vietminh hoped to bring matters to a head in Northern Laos. The French command divined their intentions and decided to cut off their lines of communication by establishing a strong point at Dien Bien Phu.

The first move was to drop six battalions of parachutists at a chosen spot in November 1953. Two months later this strong point was ready.

The Vietminh soldiers under General Giap—with five divisions, one a heavy division with field and anti-aircraft artillery and engineering equipment—quickly surrounded the depression into which the French had dug themselves. The French had also established look-outs on the surrounding hills and strengthened the wire.

Then the impossible happened. With the assistance of thousands of peasants, Giap had cut a network of hidden tracks in the dense undergrowth surrounding the French position, and along these, he brought up provisions, munitions, and even heavy artillery.

Thereafter, the strong point, which was overlooked from the surrounding hills, was shelled continuously. After several weeks of bitter fighting, the French outposts fell one by one despite the heroic resistance of Colonel de Castries's soldiers who fought to the last man and the last round of ammunition.

The fall of Dien Bien Phu had a decisive moral effect. On 20 July 1954 an armistice put an end to the cruel war in Indochina.

But now another was starting, this time in Algeria, where the rebels were preparing to throw the French out of North Africa, where they had been for more than a century.

The rebels, the *fellaghas*, secretly supported by Morocco and Tunisia, had the advantage of popular support, genuine or enforced, and, as in Indochina, the modern French units were not trained in guerrilla warfare. Under capable leaders such as General Challe, the French army nonetheless

THE MODERN FRENCH ARMY
1 30-ton AMX tank
2 Light machine-gun carrier M.16
3 AML 90 armoured car
4 AMX VTT general purpose troop carrier
5 AMX VTT seen from the rear

1

2

3

4

5

inflicted a number of severe defeats on the rebels, and soon victory was within sight. But in 1962 the Agreement of Evian ended the struggle and gave Algeria her independence; for that country had become an intolerable burden to the French union, now threatened with utter disintegration.

Since then, the war in Indochina, which has flared up again, has shown once more the difficulties that confront the American army, with the most up-to-date arms and well-trained soldiers, in the face of an elusive enemy that makes up for its lack of resources in material by its ingenuity and audacity.

The two great world powers, Russia and the United States, have replaced the "Cold War" with "peaceful coexistence". But despite all efforts towards disarmament, the great powers are committed to what is really continued arming. Every day the numbers of long-range high-speed missiles increase: intercontinental ballistic missiles, submarines, and supersonic aircraft, all capable of carrying thermonuclear missiles for great distances. This is the method thought to be the surest guarantee of peace.

This threat of atomic war has not, however, prevented local wars, such as the Vietnam war. In these wars, conventional weapons, with all the latest improvements of modern technology, are employed.

The assault tank, which will be the land-based weapon best suited to a future nuclear war, and which is now part and parcel of conventional warfare, is regularly being improved.

The British Chieftain tank is generally held to be the most powerful tank in the western world. It is armed with a 120-mm quick-firing gun with a gyroscopic stabiliser and infra-red equipment for use at night. The crew of four is protected against radio-active fall-out, and its main and auxiliary motors are "polycarburant" (they function equally well using petrol, turbine oil, or 74/80 octane spirit, [supercarburant] but will also work with a mixture of any of these). This 52-ton tank has a speed of 40 kilometres an hour, with a range of about 250 miles.

The 27-ton Vickers tank is more mobile and faster, but has less fire-power than the Chieftain. It is armed with the Swingfire anti-tank guided missile, and is able to destroy the heaviest tanks. A 13-ton Vickers tank, which is air-transportable, is at present on the drawing-board.

Starting with the AMX tank armed with the 75-mm gun, the French have developed a whole range of

MODERN ARMIES (III)
1 Russian heavy Y-55 tank
2 U.S.A. Sheridan tank
3 British Chieftain tank
4 U.S.A. 105mm self-propelled howitzer
5 U.S.A. M-113 troop carrier
6 French AMX command vehicle with aerials

1

2

3

4

5

6

armoured vehicles from troop carriers to heavy engineer equipment, and including command tanks, a 105-mm self-propelled howitzer, and an armoured ambulance. The last of the series was produced in 1963. This was the $32\frac{1}{2}$ ton AMX 30, with a speed of 65 kilometres an hour; it is armed with a British 105-mm gun. The AMX 30 is the French version of the standard European tank and is designed to operate in conditions of nuclear warfare.

Another remarkable armoured vehicle is the German 39-ton Standard tank which is armed with the same gun as the AMX 30 and has the same speed.

Naturally, Russia did not rest on her laurels, and, since the T-34, she has developed the JS-III, the T-55, and the T-10, weighing 46, 36 and 50 tons respectively. There are also battalions of decontamination vehicles for cleansing armoured fighting vehicles that have been in areas contaminated by nuclear bombs.

The USA has also considerably increased the proportion of armoured vehicles in infantry divisions. The number has grown from 72 in 1945 to 295 today. The best all-purpose tank in the US Army is the 46-ton M-60, armed with a 105-mm gun, and with a speed of 45 kilometres an hour. Another reconnaissance tank used by the USA is the 16-ton General Sheridan, armed with a 152-mm gun which can fire either nuclear or conventional shells. Its relatively light weight allows it to be dropped by parachute and to attain the remarkable speed of 70 kilometres an hour.

The American and the West German military authorities are also trying to develop a new tank intended as a general-purpose armoured fighting vehicle; hence its name Main Battle Tank, MBT.

These precautions may not sound encouraging. We can at least draw comfort from this aspect of the armaments race: that despite the menace of the H bomb there is no doubt that it is only the knowledge of the terrifying power of this weapon and its lasting effects that will prevent its use. The fear of reprisal will henceforth enforce upon possible antagonists the most profound mutual respect for one another, or so we must hope.

MODERN ARMIES (IV)
1 German F-104
2 U.S.A. F-III
3 U.S.S.R. Yakovlev
4 British F3 Lightning
5 Belgian F-104
6 Italian Fiat G-91
7 French Mirage III B
8 U.S.A. Experimental helicopter
9 U.S.A. "Nike Hercules" missile
10 U.S.A. "Sergeant" rocket
11 U.S.A. "Hawk" missiles on tracked carrier
12 Giant U.S.S.R. rocket
13 U.S.S.R. rockets on tracked carriers

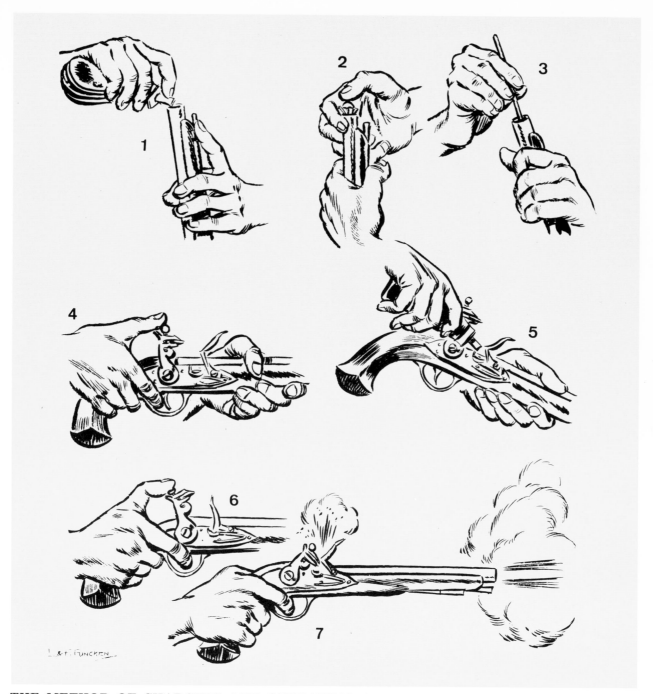

THE METHOD OF CHARGING AND OPERATING A FLINTLOCK PISTOL

1, Pour the required amount of gunpowder into the barrel. 2, Insert the bullet wrapped in a small piece of cloth into the barrel. The cloth serves to seal the projectile. 3, The ball is rammed down the barrel with a rod, pressing it firmly against the powder. 4, Lift the steel and set the cock in the safe (half-cock) position. 5, The pistol is then primed with fine powder. 6, Lower the steel and then pull the cock right back. 7, Press the trigger. When the flint hits the corrugated surface of the steel, the spark ignites the primer which fires the charge in the barrel.

THE EVOLUTION OF THE RIFLE

1350: Bronze handgun: 49.5cm

1375: Steel handgun: 56.5cm

1399: Bronze handgun: 32cm

1405: Hand mortar: 31cm

1437: *Trait a poudre* with a wrought iron shaft, approx 1m

1450: Introduction of the cock to hold the match; transition from hand igniting to the matchlock: approx 1m

1475: Martin Merz's arquebus: improved lock, and sights

1500–60: Matchlock arquebus

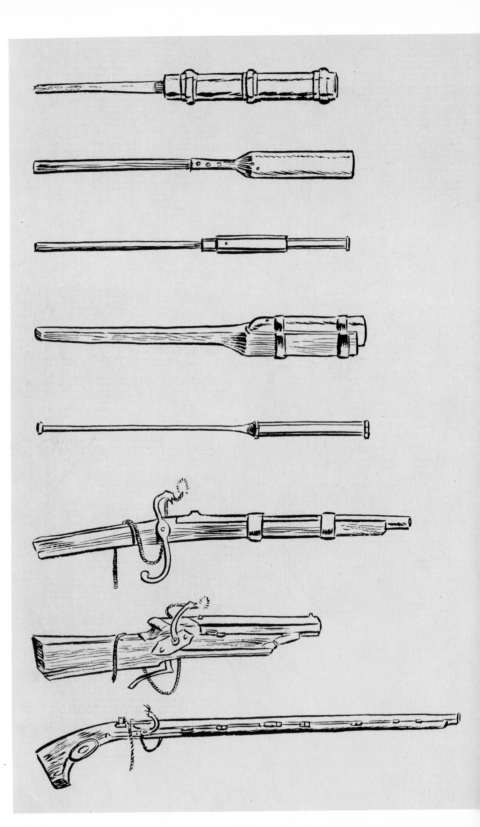

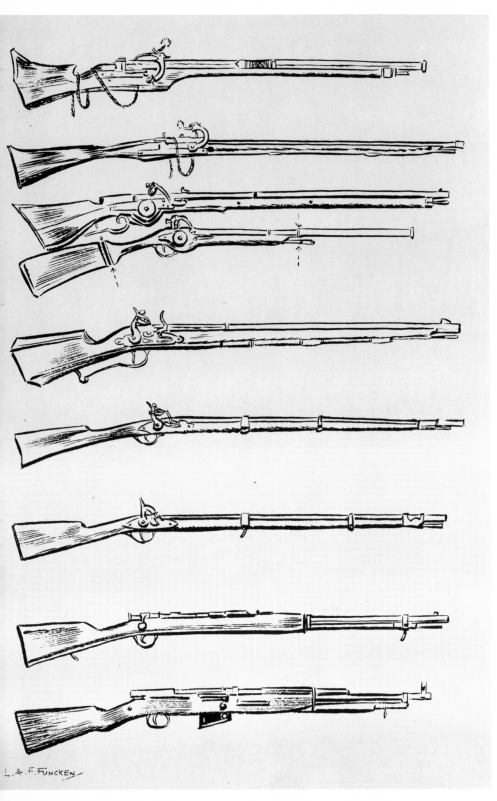

1600:   Spanish matchlock arquebus: 1.50m

1620:   English matchlock arquebus: 1.75m

1625:   Wheel-lock musket: 1.40m

1650:   French wheel-lock carbine, convertible into pistol: 1.20m

1660:   English flint-lock arquebus: 1.70m

1717:   French flint-lock musket: 1.85m

1841:   External percussion musket: 1.15m

1884:   American breech-loading internal percussion rifle: 1.15m

Present day: Russian automatic carbine, SKS: 1.20m

L. & F. FÜNCKEN

Index